SOMME INTELLIGENCE

Somme Intelligence

Fourth Army HQ 1916

Prisoner Interrogations and Captured Documents

William Langford

Pen & Sword
MILITARY

First published in Great Britain in 2013 by
Pen & Sword Military
an imprint of
Pen & Sword Books Ltd
47 Church Street
Barnsley
South Yorkshire
S70 2AS

ISBN 9781781590829

Typeset in Palatino 10pt by Factionpress

Printed and bound by CPI Group (UK) Ltd, Croydon, CR0 4YY

Pen & Sword Books Ltd incorporates the Imprints of Pen & Sword Aviation, Pen & Sword
Maritime, Pen & Sword Military, Wharncliffe Local History, Pen & Sword Select, Pen &
Sword Military Classics and Leo Cooper.
For a complete list of Pen & Sword titles please contact
PEN & SWORD BOOKS LIMITED
47 Church Street, Barnsley, South Yorkshire, S70 2AS, England
E-mail: enquiries@pen-and-sword.co.uk
Website: www.pen-and-sword.co.uk

Contents

Introduction

The very first recorded intelligence gathering brief in history is available to us in some detail. The 3,500-year-old record contains the following instructions to agents selected to carry out a dangerous fact-finding mission:

Go north from here into the southern part of the land... then into the hill country. Find out what kind of country it is, how many people live there, and how strong they are. Find out whether the land is good or bad and whether the people live in open towns or in fortified cities. Find out whether the soil is fertile and whether the land is wooded.

The commander of the army about to invade needed detailed information, even ordering the spies to bring back samples of produce. See Numbers Chapter 13, verses 18, 19, 20 of the Bible.

So it would be throughout time, whenever men formed into armed camps and warred against each other, accurate information concerning the other's circumstances would become necessary. In instances where one of the belligerents failed to gather sufficient intelligence about the enemy, or where gathered reports were ignored or down-played, the ordinary foot soldier has paid the price. For example, Saturday 1 July 1916, proved to be the most catastrophic day in the history of the British Army, with over 19,000 men killed and around 35,500 wounded. Added to these were the missing and those taken prisoner, making the mind-numbing total of 57,470 as an estimate. The optimistic attitude of the British generals, the planners of that disaster, caused them to be selective in their assessments of the accumulating intelligence arriving on their desks in the lead up to the offensive. They were well aware that the type of German positions they were assaulting had very deep underground shelters where the defenders were safe against the week-long preparatory bombardment. Further, despite the shelling, there were reports that German barbed wire entanglements still remained unbroken on most sections of the 15-mile-long front. That intelligence was either disregarded or played down. German deserters, and prisoners taken in trench raids, complained to their interrogators of terrible conditions the Germans troops were experiencing because of the shelling. British Fourth Army HQ, tasked with mounting the Somme offensive, would certainly have been encouraged by this sort of report; discounting the known tendency of the rank and file of all nations to be bitter complainers and prone to woefully exaggerating their lot in life. Also, and understandably, some warriors who fall into enemy hands are more than ready to tell their captors what they believe their questioners would prefer to hear.

The last time British forces lost men out-rivalling the figure of those killed in one day in the Battle of the Somme, was during the Wars of the Roses. Following the Battle of Towton, in Yorkshire in 1461, the heralds counted, in round figures, 28,000 dead after nine hours fighting. This of course was a civil war when rival kings fought for the throne of England. Civil wars have a notorious reputation for being especially brutal as those, once neighbours, exact revenge for perceived past grievances and grasp an opportunity to re-open old feuds. Further, it is difficult to know who is the enemy in these circumstances, as even members of the same family could harbour opposing views. Betrayal and 'turning the coat' during the fighting in the fifteenth century was commonplace. There can be no question that spies and agents were active gathering intelligence during the Wars of the Roses, but the medieval chronicles do not directly refer to this. However, events during that conflict indicate that clandestine activity was rife. For example, during the Battle of Northampton in 1460, the right wing of the Lancastrian line of defenders under the command of Lord Grey, suddenly laid down their weapons and helped the attacking Yorkists through the barrier of stakes. That betrayal caused the Yorkists to be victorious; the defection having been arranged beforehand through agents. This led to the capture of Lancastrian King Henry VI.

It was that English king's grandson, Henry VIII, who later defined the role of an appointed chief 'reconnoitier' of the army – the 'Scoutmaster'. The position of Scoutmaster came more to the fore in the English Civil War (1642 to 1651) when both sides fielded an overseer of agents. Enemy troop movements were observed along with the numbers being employed; discipline, logistics, equipment and morale were also noted and reported on. Spies for Oliver Cromwell, under the oversight of the Scoutmaster, were installed in the homes of known Royalists, in the streets and markets and even in the Royalist court when in exile. After the restoration the Scoutmaster designation was changed to that of Quarter Master General.

At the beginning of the next century an English army under the command of the Duke of Marlborough employed the services of Quarter Master General, William Cadogan. This was against the French in the Wars of the Spanish Succession (1702 to 1713). During the campaign in Europe the Quarter Master General moved ahead of the army and recruited guides to aid with intelligence gathering. Agents were ensconced within the French court and supplied crucial information on the movements and intentions of the French army.

Later in the eighteenth century european nations became embroiled in, what would be termed, the Seven Years War (1756 to 1763). British General Wolf, in his planning to capture Quebec from the French, personally undertook the intelligence work, interrogating deserters,

William Cadogan, 1st Earl Cadogan
1675 – 1726.

questioning his scouts (known as 'Rangers'), interpreting intercepted messages and even conducting his own reconnaissance.

Subsequent British failures on the American continent could be attributed, to some degree, to poor intelligence work and resulted in the loss to the Crown of those colonies – War of American Independence (1775 to 1783).

Learning lessons from defeat, the British Army in the Peninsular War (1808 to 1814), shaped-up and the beginnings of military intelligence as is understood in the present day took place. When British general Sir John Moore advanced on Salamanca then withdrew to Corunna, informing him all the while was a locally recruited Peninsula Corps of Guides. Under Arthur Wellesley (later to become the Duke of Wellington) that organization was formally established in 1809. The Corps of Guides began with a complement of six officers and thirty-eight operatives. Numbers increased as French deserters were recruited and Portuguese officers added. The work undertaken was that of interpreting, tactical questioning, reconnaissance, making maps and sketches of terrain and, most importantly, shadowing enemy movements and counting his forces (usually done at river crossings). Agents belonging to the Corps of Guides operated deep within enemy occupied territory. One British officer, Captain Scovell, was successful in decoding intercepted French despatches.

Arthur Wellesley, 1st Duke of Wellington 1769–1852.

Following the defeat of Napoleon at Waterloo there was a decline in the art of intelligence gathering. By that time the Corps of Guides had been disbanded it having been deemed purely a Peninsular requirement for the British Army at that time. Not until the war in the Crimea in 1854 was there a conflict demanding the employment of an intelligence service of the merit of the Corps of Guides.

When Lord Raglan, Commander of the British Army, landed in the Crimea to fight the Russians he was to employ a civilian intelligence gatherer by the name of Calvert. However, his services ended abruptly when the man died of cholera in 1855. Poor administration of the British Army in the Crimea and faulty logistical support is now legendary; inadequate intelligence gleaning was a part of the overall malaise. By the end of that conflict brought about by the capture of Sebastopol in 1856, Britain's reputation among the European nations had suffered a severe blow.

Up to the end of that century the wars engaged in by the British Army were, in the main, against natives armed with edged weapons. At the outset of the Zulu War, 1879, intelligence was left to a civilian who had produced a detailed manual which contained warnings of what the British would be coming up against. The British,

under the command of Lord Chelmsford, treated the intelligence with contempt and suffered a defeat at Isandlwana, following which Chelmsford usefully employed scouts from the Natal Volunteers.

Three years later, with the Egyptian expedition in view, useful information gathering was done by a young Kitchener and a Major Tulloch supposedly engaged on a shooting trip. When the campaign in the Sudan began small intelligence staffs reconnoitered, interrogated captives and controlled agents. Because of his involvement in the earlier intelligence gathering, Kitchener, when he became Commander-in-Chief, made sure that an efficient service was put in place. This proved its worth and employed disinformation to mislead the Khalifa before the Battle of Omdurman in 1898.

For the Boer War in South Africa in 1899 failure to have the correct information available caused disaster in the opening stages. The Commander-in-Chief, Sir George White, had no inkling of the importance of intelligence gathering and was soon besieged at Ladysmith. Out to assist came General Redvers Buller, likewise

Horatio Herbert Kitchener, 1st Earl Kitchener 1850-1916.

without the benefit of an intelligence service and was promptly defeated at the Battle of Colenso. Incredibly, the most detailed work on the South African situation existed and was available to the commanders. Major General Sir John Ardagh and his Intelligence Division back in London had, in a published report, identified the possible enemy in that region of Africa and flagged up the purchase of up-to-date Mauser rifles from Germany by the Boer states. The handbook produced by Ardagh's department gave the number of machine guns, artillery, the amount of munitions and the number of men available to the Boer leaders. It was military incompetence of the highest order not to have consulted this, and taken it into planning strategy when hostilities erupted. The ordinary British soldier suffered the consequences at such battles that took place on the Spion Kop.

Major General Sir John Charles Ardagh 1840-1907.

When Lord Roberts took over, after the removal of Buller following the Colenso disaster, he arrived in South Africa with his own Head of Intelligence, Colonel George Henderson, who formed the Field Intelligence Department FID, developed the operation until it numbered 132 officers and over 2,000 white soldiers plus native scouts. Knowledge of Boer strengths, morale, likely courses of action, weapons and equipment greatly aided British military headquarters. When hostilities ended Henderson firmed up the intelligence operation by writing a manual *Field Intelligence, Its Principles and Practices* and recommended the forming of an Intelligence Corps. In the light of his experience gained in the field he was able to include in his manual the type of character looked for in intelligence officers:

The successful intelligence officer must be cool, courageous, and adroit, patient and imperturbable, discreet and trustworthy. He must understand the handling of troops and have a knowledge of the art of war. He must be able to win the confidence of his general, and to inspire confidence in his subordinates. He must have resolution to continue unceasingly his search for information, even in the most disheartening circumstances and after repeated failures.

He must have endurance to submit silently to criticism, much of which may be based on ignorance or jealousy. And he must be able to deal with men, to approach his source of information with tact and skill, whether such source be a patriotic gentleman or an abandoned traitor.

Lieutenant Colonel David Henderson 1862-1921.

Field Intelligence by Lieutenant Colonel David Henderson. Page 1

Declaration of War by the British Empire, August 1914

At General Headquarters there was a determination to avoid past unpreparedness in matters of military awareness of enemy plans and intentions. When elements of the British Expeditionary Force crossed the Channel aboard SS *Olympia*, 13 August 1914, members of the Intelligence Corps were aboard the same transport. In command of the new corps, appointed in September, was a Major Archibald Wavell who would later become Field Marshal Lord Wavell. Being a regular soldier he, like many of his fellow officers, struggled to come to terms with the largely undisciplined forty or more intelligence officers under his charge. They had been recruited, encouraged to join, or volunteered to serve in the Intelligence Corps because they spoke either French or German and were capable of riding a horse and motorcycle. They were viewed as amateurs with little work to do and prejudice against them abounded. Within weeks Wavell managed to secure a posting to 9 Infantry Brigade and away from the disliked and frowned upon ad hoc intelligence unit.

However, at GHQ work a-plenty was found for the Intelligence Corps operatives, there was much to oversee and check out; intelligence officers were attached to cavalry units, also to the Royal Flying Corps, engaged in battlefield reconnaissance. They were soon embroiled in security, secret service work, censorship and even public relations, which was aimed at the civilian population (French and British) and British troops. As the Great War stretched out over the months and years the Corps took on prisoner interrogation, aerial photograph interpretation, censorship, document translation, propaganda and counter espionage.

It was under the leadership of Major Sir John Dunnington-Jefferson, who was appointed Commandant of the Intelligence Corps in December 1914, and who developed the arm until February 1916, that the corps' reputation became well established on the Western Front. For the period of the Battle of the Somme – and until the end of the war – Captain A. A. Fenn commanded the corps.

Recording information for use by GHQ Staff Officers

For the Somme offensive, British Fourth Army headquarters was situated in a chateau at Querrieu on the Albert-Amiens road. In the build up months to Haig's Great Push a steady flow of intelligence was being compiled; captured German documents, intercepted messages, prisoners' letters, diaries and information gleaned from prisoner interviews were entered into foolscap-size ledgers where they could be perused by the planners.

The hand-written journal of intelligence reports upon which this work is formed was originally compiled by a former soldier of the 11th Battalion, East Lancashire Regiment, (Accrington Pals), Harry Platt of Burnley. In 1916 he was a sergeant working on intelligence duties at

Harry Platt, December 1914.

Fourth Army GHQ. He was later commissioned in the Royal Engineers. Harry also served in the Second World War in the Royal Artillery reaching the rank of Major. He was Mentioned in Despatches in both conflicts. Harry died in August 1951 aged 56.

In 2002 the handwritten journal was lodged with the Imperial War Museum at the instigation of historian William Turner, military historian and author of books on the Accrington Pals.

As the reader goes through these reports it would be helpful to keep in mind that members of the British staff at Querrieu chateau, including Generals Haig and Rawlinson, would have had their impressions coloured by the words you are reading and doubtless their optimism for a successful outcome to the Somme offensive greatly enhanced. They would have noted the effect the British bombardment was having; dominance of the Royal Flying Corps as its machines seemingly operated unmolested over the trenches; growing unrest in German cities as food shortages drove the populace to riot; and the relentless call-up to the colours of ever-younger youths as that nation's manhood bled in the great battles taking place.

Bibliography
British Military Intelligence by Jock Haswell, Weidenfeld and Nicolson, 1973
Forearmed – A History of the Intelligence Corps by Anthony Clayton, Brassey's 1993
The Intelligencers by Brigadier Brian Parritt, Pen & Sword Books, 2011
Wavell – Soldier & Statesman by Victoria Schofield, Pen & Sword Books, 2010

General Headquarters Intelligence Staff in 1916
Top: Captain E. W. Shepherd, Royal Engineers; Captain Stewart Menzies; Lieutenant Colonel Church; unidentified; Major Sir John Dunnington-Jefferson; Major J. H. M. Cornwall, Royal Artillery.
Seated: Lieutenant Colonel E. M. Jack, Royal Engineers; Lieutenant Colonel Walter Kirke, Royal Artillery; Brigadier General John Charteris, Royal Engineers; Lieutenant Colonel B. W. Bowdler, Royal Engineers; Lieutenant Colonel H. D. Goldsmith, Duke of Cornwall's Light Infantry.
Right: Major A. H. Hutton-Wilson (absent for the group photograph).

Chapter One

An Der Somme

Examination of captured documents checked and passed to Fourth Army HQ

From the examination of captured German documents the following information has been obtained:

6 October 1915

It was noted that during the battle of Loos that rifles that had been exposed to English poison gas clouds began to show signs of rust. Rifles must therefore be cleaned and oiled as soon as such a gas cloud has passed our trenches.

British soldiers on a work detail wearing the cape the Germans wished to examine. It is referred to as a 'greatcoat' rather than 'cape' – perhaps something lost in translation.

12 October 1915

According to an announcement by the War Office the British War Office has again approved a new type of greatcoat for the English troops. This coat can be used, as the case may be, as a water-proof coat, a sleeping-bag, a ground-sheet, apron, or valise covering. In case such a greatcoat is found it is to be handed in to the Divisional Headquarters.

2 February 1916

At home in Germany they require empty bottles and tins. At the Front all troops and town authorities must deliver empty bottles to the canteen and empty tins to the collecting place in Bapaume.

They must report by 20 February 1916 how many bottles and tins they have collected between the days 15 February and 19 February.

Attention is again drawn to the directive that all parings from horses hoofs are to be collected and are to be handed in to the smith's stores in Bapaume. This has not been done by all troops yet.

Bapaume was the main town behind the lines on the Somme. Chalked on the artillery shell is the date: 19 August 1916 – height of the Somme Battle. Shortage of raw materials in Germany is seen in the above call for empty bottles and tins. Even the parings of the hooves of horses are to be collected for the manufacture of glue.

Extract from a captured diary

27 February 1916

Snow thawing. Everybody in the trench is wet and ill of late. Supply has again become very bad. Only a good supply of marmalade. In the infantry two more men deserted and left behind a note 'We can't carry on on marmalade.' Truly a sign of a bad spirit that animates us.

29 February 1916

Heroism, which lives only on ideals and in the realms of thought, quickly fails for want of breath. Ten days in position and the food we get is a bit too much.

Speech of His Majesty the Emperor and King

To the 3rd Guard Infantry Division in the Champagne, on their arrival from the Eastern Front.

20 April 1916

I greet the several units composing the 3rd Guard Infantry Division, in the Western Theatre of war. In the course of this campaign the 3rd Guard Division has, to my great satisfaction, hitherto performed splendid deeds, such as are in conformity with its composition and its origin. The heavy battles in the Carpathian mountains, the advance until the approach of winter, the combats in the positions held during the winter – all are inscribed on the long scroll in the glorious history of the several regiments. The *fusileers*, with the exception of a deputation near Brezezany, I have not seen since the spring of 1914, not since the days when you were at Döberitz. You have now displayed before the enemy, under all conditions, what you have learned to my satisfaction and joy, during the many years of peace. For this, as your one time commander, I express to you my appreciation. In accordance with my orders you have come from the East to the West, you the 'Cockchafers' of the Army to herald to the enemy the approach of a martial spring season.

The Lehr Infantry Regiment, I greet today for the first time in its present composition. It has evolved from the Battalion which is, so to speak,   *Kaiser Wilhelm II.*

the prototype of my entire Army, which from olden times has held the honour of guarding the King, his house and family, and is in daily contact with his person, which is the connecting link between the Guard of the Prussian Army as a whole. In conformity with its lofty military origin, the bearing of this regiment in battle has been blameless. My congratulations!

And you Kolbergers! We have already met once in the East. Now I have brought you over here. The heroism you have displayed shall never be forgotten. You have dictated law, writ in iron, unto the enemy, who will not soon forget the butt-end of your Pomeranian rifles. Siemikawce remains a glorious and honoured page in the annals of your Regiment, as also the battles of the Carpathians and on the Zwinin. They will always be linked with the history of my 'Cockchafers' Regiment.

The Kaiser with officers on the Somme front 1916.

The other units which belong to this division, the cavalry and artillery, especially the artillery, have in these strenuous fights given the infantry that assistance, which in this war I must expect for my infantry, without fail.

The entire division has thus been summoned by my orders to this front in splendid condition and with an excellent record of active service. It is now in the west to do its share in the great task, in the overwhelming of our enemies. The foe fights differently over here, defending his native soil foot by foot, which we must put to his credit. This is the resistance of despair. But it must be broken. He has prepared his own soup and now he must sup it, and I look to you to see to it. May the appearance of the 3rd Guard Infantry Division convey to the enemy what kind of soldiers are facing him, and may the good God who has stood by everyone of you in many an hour of trial lead you to victory. May he lead you to the peace we all desire. I count on your help.

Note: The Guard *Fusileer* Regiment is nicknamed the 'Cockchafers' (*Maikäfer*) after the May beetle.

Extracts from letters

21 April 1916

Elberfeld

There was heavy fighting where he was but here, nothing is happening because you cannot get anything. We no longer get sausage and meat, by that you can see what is happening here. Fourteen days ago the women here stormed the Town Hall and scolded the mayor. Several of the women were arrested and this sort of thing happens every day. At every place of sale there are police and thousands of purchasers.

Dear Otto, The hermit from Ostersiegen is dead. He appears to have died from starvation.

Dear Otto, Here at home there is nothing much happening, because you cannot get anything more for money. There is in fact no more meat. For that reason it is time that the war should come to an end.

Extract from a letter written in Nuremberg

25 April 1916

Today we have had to fill up a form showing what store of provisions we have in the house. But we have no stocks in these hard times. We now have sugar and meat cards; but I hardly ever cook meat now. Beef costs 2/6d a lb, veal and lamb 2/- and 1/11d. How can one eat meat at this price?

Local defence of battery positions

30 April 1916

The following is taken from an Order of the 11th Division:

All batteries in front of the Second line will be provided with thick, deep barbed wire entanglement extending round the flanks of the battery. This entanglement will be sufficiently close to the guns to allow grenades to be thrown beyond it, that is, about twenty yards. Carbines, rifles and revolvers, as well as grenades, must be kept handy for close fighting; they must not be left in dug-outs when the detachment is at the guns.

As the British blocade of the Central Powers bit deep, flower beds in German cities and towns were sown with vegetables. Here in Berlin citizens plant salad beds.

Extract from a letter sent from Lichtenberg

12 June 1916

Everything is awfully expensive. Mother says things have never been so dear in her lifetime before. Bread and meat she has always had... Do you still have meat? There will be no meat in July and August and if you come on leave you will get no meat here.

German bread ration book. The harvest for 1916 was poor making the food situation worse.

Extracts from the diary of an officer of the 127th Infantry Regiment, XIII Corps. Left Ypres front

29 July for the Somme

Written during the bombardment before the Canadian attack at Hill 60, on 13 June.

12 June 1916

The 125th Regiment is positioned next to us. I heard that an entire squad of them said that they would not go forward any longer. They had better be shot here then, and so there would be no need to carry them back. Certainly the artillery fire is absolutely awful, but I would never have thought such disobedience to orders possible. Rumours that have reached the 127th that men of the 125th would not attack anymore are now confirmed.

Cooking arrangements

15 June 1916

1. Cooking courses ordered by the Regiment are to take place at once under direction of the Battalion doctors or their deputies.
2. The Battalion doctor will, with the Commissariat Officer of the Battalion and the three Company Feldwebel at present in Montauban, arrange a menu on the basis of the present existing three-day scheme, and cook accordingly.
3. I must call to notice that it is absolutely indispensable to the potato supply that those be peeled very thinly or, as higher authorities wish, that they be cooked in their skins.
4. Further, flour at present abundant, is to be put to useful account.
5. It will be left to experience, whether to introduce entirely meatless days, or to distribute equally the supplied meat over several days. Let it be noted here that the food must always be solid – not merely broth.
6. I am ready to grant any demands for more spices to strengthen

A German field bakery in operation on the Somme.

the foods and with reference to this point, the respective demands
and wishes must be handed in by Saturday evening.

7. Finally, I call attention to the sowing and laying out of vegetables
and salad beds by the companies as ordered.

8. I request the doctor to report in writing by 1 July, on the results
and any further wants he may require.

Extracts from captured letters to German soldiers

21 June 1916

The military had to assist in restoring order with loaded firearms.
The women are neither afraid of sabres, rifles, knuckle-dusters or
horses.

To a soldier from his wife

Zwota

Dear Paul,

You will have heard by now that the Russians have again invaded
Galacia; they have captured 100,000 Austrians and also Germans in
two weeks. I believe we also will be destroyed, because if this
continues the enemy will soon be in our Fatherland. It can't make
much difference to us if we are Germans or if we must belong to
some other nation, so long as they make all the highly placed people
in our nation the servants, because only they wanted the war.

Dear Paul you can't believe what a lot of troops have come to Austria, all of them are Saxons. If someone is in distress the Saxons have to go forward. They it is who will put everything in order. If they were all like Saxons and Bavarians the war could have been ended long ago.

20 June 1916

Munich

My dearest F...,

Your kind letter I received with thanks. I will readily tell you of the current rumour: It is that the 16th Regiment [16th Bavarian?] had mutinied and that the Kaiser wished every tenth man to be shot. The Crown Prince [presumably of Bavaria] however, wired that he would go for the Prussians with his regiment. Just write 'yes' or 'no' in order that it passes the Censor, as such rumours get on one's nerves.

Dearest F...,

You cannot imagine what crowds there were on Saturday and Sunday in Marienplatz [Munich]. Thousands of people collected at the Rathaus [Town hall] and chanted for bread. They smashed all the windows in the café and Rathaus and all the neighbouring shops and business premises. The women carried on exactly like young hooligans. The mounted police and others had to draw and use their sabres. Many people were injured and the police had a very rough time of it.

A pre-war postcard of Marienplatz, Munich, the scene of food riots in June 1916.

German letter written from Mönsheim dated

26 June 1916

My dear Brother,

So glad to get your letter. Are you ever going to get leave? I hear from Willy that he can't get leave to come back here, and I did not see him last time because one has no desire to travel in these times. Here, at home, everything is as before but oh! if only this horrible war were at an end. Just the last few days troops have been going from France to Russia to help over there again. There seems to be no end to this war.

Worms railway station and the booking hall where the food riot took place in June 1916.

Below: Bread card. The card entitles the holder to purchase 14 pounds of bread or 10 pounds and 3 pounds of bread flour also $^1/_2$ pounds of rice. New cards will not be issued for those lost or any cards used too early.

A few days ago there was a great row in Worms. It began in the morning when the people wanted to buy things in the market, strange dealers had already taken everything to the railway. The crowd went to the station, stripped everything from the wagons and trod underfoot everything they could not carry away. Then about mid-day a few thousand people gathered in the market place and shouted 'Famine' etc. They continued into the evening and they attacked a few shops in the Rafergasse, broke the shop windows etc. They took all the clothes from a Jew's shop. They railed at the Chief of Police properly. I believe that he is very unpopular. It was only when the military appeared and opened fire that the crowd dispersed, but we hear that today the riots are continuing. They have closed off the street. It was mostly women, but this is understandable, the feeling is too strong, for the people in the town cannot continue to live anymore. The district of Worms is supposed to be one of the worst and very little care is taken there.

Please send me, my dear brother, some jelly and cheese; one cannot obtain sufficient here otherwise. Now good luck and best love from us all.

Your loving sister.

Extract of a letter written from Munich
27 June 1916

Addressed to a lance corporal in the 16th Bavarian Infantry Regiment.

Never have there been such troubled times as these. There is frightful exasperation and discontent amongst the people. Each one thinks that he may go short. Such times will not occur again easily. You have to struggle for meat, eggs, potatoes etc., as you might for a kingdom. You have perhaps heard of the gathering of the people at the Marienplatz as you mentioned it in your last letter. In the Town Hall and the Town Hall Café they broke several windows. Tram traffic was entirely stopped as the people were standing shoulder to shoulder. At first there were only women clamouring for bread cards. In the evening they were joined by men coming home from their work. From the Town Hall café water was poured on the excited mob and small pieces of bread were thrown from the windows. That was the last straw. The riot is said to have lasted until three in the morning. There is very little mention of it in the papers. The people ought to have done more damage than they did,

Ration card for bread or flour.

German citizens reading the latest directive from the town's military governor.

Berlin, the German capital, children at an orphanage being served their war-time diet of soup.

because the Authorities would rather let everything go to rack and ruin than give it to the 'motley crowd' as they call the people. You have no idea what ferment there is among the population. They are only waiting for you men to start properly. The military have already been called out once or twice. The people have already once or twice given the *Wohrkraftjungen* a thorough thrashing because they are so quick to shoot.

Next week I will send you a parcel. This week I am not able to get any sausage or cheese, everything is promised but nothing is obtainable. I cannot bake any cakes for you as I am not able to procure any sugar or flour, and one cannot buy cakes anymore.

Many a time I would rather bang my head against a wall than see and hear any more of this.

Practically all German boys from the age of 15 to 18 join a Corps named the *Wohrkraftjungen* which is something similar to the English Cadet Corps or Boy Scouts.

Effects of British bombardment

16 June 1916

The enemy artillery does not forget to send us greetings at night as well as by day. They seem to know our dug-outs better than we do ourselves.

20 June 1916

11th Reserve Regiment XIV Reserve Corps   (Fricourt Sector)
We are quite shut off from the rest of the world; nothing comes up to us; no letters. The English keep such a barrage on all approaches; it's terrible. Tomorrow morning it will be seven days since the bombardment began; we cannot hold out much longer; everything is shot to pieces.

20 June 1916

1st Battalion 111st Reserve Regiment XIV Reserve Corps (Fricourt Sector)
Written to a fellow soldier employed at 28th Reserve Division Post Office, Bapaume.
Heavy fire since 24th inst. Our casualties are, I am glad to say, quite small. In our Company for example, there have been none killed. No attack so far; any way we are prepared. Our artillery are doing splendidly. If the shell fire does not drive you out of Bapaume there is no need to move on account of the English; they won't get as far as that.

Smashed up ground at Fricourt caused by the week-long British artillery bombardment in preparation for the 'Big Push'.

Diary probably also Fricourt sector

25 June 1916

Bombardment continued all day, impossible to fetch rations. After dark a party hurried up to the church and brought back some stew.

27 June 1916

Report of Platoon Commander to Officer Commanding Company 9/109th Reserve Regiment.

I have the impression that the artillery could not give sufficient support. Enemy mortars have been systematically firing at each of our dug-outs with the aid of aerial observation, (less so today). They have been able to handle their mortars as if on exercise and have not been engaged at all by our artillery. I also noticed today that when artillery fire was called for, on our left the reply was late and, in comparison to the enemy fire, very weak.

Leutnant Cazarus

The church at Fricourt before and after the British bombardment.

29 June 1916

Our thirst is terrible, we hunt for and drink the water in shell holes.

30 June 1916

Report to 9th Company, 109th Reserve Regiment.

Unable to send to fetch the coffee. Will the Company Commander please make efforts to get the Battalion to send down some water the men are suffering very much from thirst. Every one of us in these five days has become years older. We hardly know ourselves. Bechtel said that in these five days he lost ten pounds. Hunger and thirst have also contributed their share to that. Hunger would be easily borne, but the thirst made one almost mad. Luckily it rained yesterday and the water in the shell holes, mixed with yellow shell sulphur, tasted as good as a bottle of beer.

Food, and more importantly water, being brought up to the front line during the summer of 1916.

Remains of the German munitions train which exploded at Combles railway station. Mention of this is found in the captured diary (below).

Extracts from a German soldier's diary

24 June 1916

The sound of gun-fire becomes progressively louder. Many shells were now falling into Combles, a very sad sight. Incendiary shells were also fired into the town and one blew up our ammunition depot.

25 June 1916

We worked until 6 am and then marched back to Raucourt. Enemy aircraft are much more active than ours. It is incomprehensible why the enemy are so daring and ours so timid. At 4 pm a French aviator attacked our three captive balloons and, incredible as it seems, brought them down. At 10 pm we paraded and marched off at 10.15 pm to the Redoubt, where we began work at 11.30 pm.

26 June 1916

We worked until 3 am. Combles is shelled unceasingly; every minute a shell, sometimes two. At 4 am the order came to march off by side roads through Combles towards the front line trenches. We

Resting during a march to the trenches.

have to pass through the outskirts of Combles – what destruction. We pass through the town in quick time. The houses that have not been wrecked are deserted.

We arrive in the trenches tired and exhausted about 5.30 am. I shall never forget the firing on the front line. We learn from orderlies that food and drink are in short supply. This is a pity, for the English offensive has been known long enough to permit more arrangements being made to prevent this. But mistakes are being made everywhere.

Measures to combat smoke attacks

Translation from an extract of a Company report to Headquarters 62nd Regiment. Proposed course of action to deal with British smoke attack.

Troops arriving at Combles Marie (town hall) and entering through the cellars into the catacombs.

28 June 1916

1. 8.30 am. A smoke attack was made by the enemy similar to that of yesterday.

2. As was the case of yesterday, the expected barrage fire of our artillery completely failed us. Six red flares were sent up, but no counter barrage fire followed.

3. On account of the very thick cloud which results during a smoke attack, it is quite impossible for the infantry in the first line to observe the enemy leaving his trenches.

4. In consequence of this, I again urgently beg that our artillery be ordered that, on observing a smoke attack or an infantry signal for barrage fire, the front enemy trenches be subjected to a concentrated fire. For should the enemy succeed in getting out of his trenches, we would not notice him until he was a matter of yards from our own positions.

Extract from a letter to an officer of the 190th Regiment

28 June 1916

Hulheim [Ruhr]

Dear Mr A,

I am curious to know if you have become stouter or thinner. Here all are thin owing to the many meatless and fatless days. It is really wretched. One is often inclined to laugh in spite of the misery, to see how people have to stand from 3 o'clock in the morning for a few grammes of fat or potatoes. The poor people suffer, children cry for bread but there is none. I could write you lots of this sort of thing but fear I should bore you.

Extract from a letter

28 June 1916

Oberlungwitz [Saxony]

Dear Paul,

We gather from your letter that you expect to be away for a year more. That would be too terrible. We are praying with anxiety for a speedy peace, for there is very severe want with us now. We have almost nothing at all to eat. The present times are bad for potatoes are almost all we get. We get three kilos per head per week. Just imagine how we must make this last out. Vegetables are hardly to be had. We get instead a little more bread, but it is not enough. We are anxious to see how it all will end.

Dear Paul,

We have a request to put to you. When you come home on leave, could you possibly bring a little meat with you for us. We would gladly give you something else in return. Most others bring a lot with them, as much as they can manage.

Extracts from letters

28 June 1916

Thank God I reached my Company in safety after going through heavy artillery fire. Since Saturday 24th, the whole 6th Company front has been bombarded without letup. Everything is shattered and houses are burning. Two comrades badly wounded. It looks terrible here as for five days and nights the artillery fire continues to a depth of ten kilometres behind the trenches; everything is blown to bits. The English want to crush us with artillery fire. Many of the dug-outs are blown in and only a few are intact. There are many dead and wounded and very many have been buried in the dug-outs.

Do not write again until I tell you as letters are now being stopped. We are not safe for one hour. Something could happen at any moment.

30 June 1916

We are in a beastly hole. The English have been shelling day and night since Saturday 24 June. They started at 7 o'clock in the morning, simply terrible, not only at us but along the whole front. We hear that it is the same at Arras where they are preparing to attack. They have already been driven back once by our neighbouring regiments. Three times this morning they sent gas over. We are getting no rest day or night. Sleep is quite a secondary thing, and as for food, that is the same; we do

Battered trench and dug-out called Point 110.

not get anything except a little coffee. Yesterday evening my NCO and other men returned empty-handed after missing their way. Yesterday, at night, they tried again to get food. This morning at 7 o'clock they returned with some coffee. I managed to get a cup full and then the man who was carrying it fell down the dug-out steps, and we had to drink it down there. Now we must wait again until tomorrow morning until we can get some more. If the 'Push' had not come we were to have been relieved on the 28th. Now we have to stick it out.

They have been shelling for 144 hours up to this morning and they are continuing. Let us hope that it will come to a stop soon. We have heard that they intend to shell us for a week.

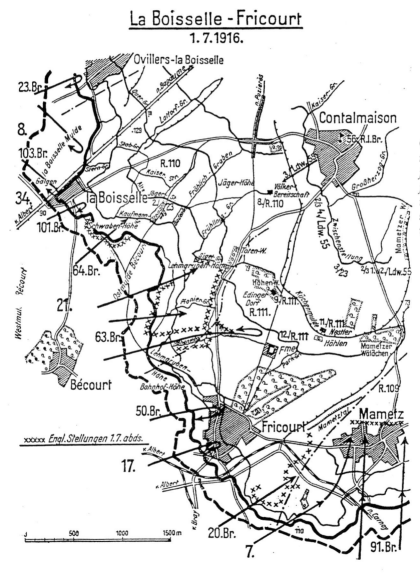

La Boisselle - Fricourt
1. 7. 1916.

German official history map depicting the fighting along the front from La Boisselle in the north to Mametz in the south and including the village of Fricourt.

Chapter Two

The Allied Attack – July 1916

Enemy losses diary entries
Saturday 1st July
During the night 30th June – 1st July, the 111th Battalion made an attack and was completely routed, had no leadership and the whole of 10th Company were taken prisoner.

Sunday 2nd July
Frightful fire on the front line, 30 cm trench mortars.

Tuesday 4th July
Relieved at 3 pm.

Thursday 6th July
To-day we go forward again – a bad prospect, for a part of the 7th Company has already been forced to evacuate their trenches. We have too little artillery support and there are no aeroplanes to be seen. The enemy planes are constantly over our trenches. Have been in the listening post with Emil Schlotz. Relieved in the night.

Extract from the diary of the officer commanding 16th Bavarian Regiment, 10th Bavarian Division.
2 July 1916
I assembled the battalion commanders and explained the situation from the information I had received from Divisional HQ. The position became even more critical because it afterwards transpired that the 6th Bavarian Reserve Regiment, which on 1 July was thrown into Montauban, had been completely wiped out. Of 3,500 men there were only 500 survivors. They were for the most part, men who had not taken part in the battle. There remained also two regimental officers and a few stragglers who turned up the following day. All the rest are dead, wounded or missing; only a small fraction fell as prisoners into the enemy's hands. The regimental staffs and battalion staffs were all captured in their dug-outs.

A captured German order
The following secret order was issued at some date in July by General von Below, commanding the Second Army:

July 1916
Secret

Second Army
Ia/802

In spite of my orders forbidding the voluntary evacuation of positions (General Order of 3 July 1916, Ia/575, Secret) certain positions in our line appear to have been abandoned before any attack had been delivered by the enemy. Every commanding officer will be held responsible if the units under his command do not fight to the last man in the sector allotted to them. Any infraction of this order will immediately render the officer concerned liable to a Court Martial. This order will be communicated to every commanding officer.

Signed v. Below.

General Fritz Wilhelm Theodor Karl von Below (centre) with the Second Army Staff in the late summer of 1916. Army commander General der Infanterie Fritz von Below is flanked by his two principal general staff officers, Oberst Fritz von Lossberg, Chief of Staff and Oberstleutnant Konrad von Redern, Quartermaster.

Translation of a German army order
Second Army order

3 July 1916

The final outcome of the war depends upon the victory of the Second Army on the Somme. We must win the battle despite the enemy's momentary superiority in guns and infantry. The important ground captured by the enemy at certain points will be retaken from them by our attacks after reinforcements have arrived. For the moment it is essential to hold our present position regardless of cost and to improve them by small counter-attacks. I forbid the voluntary evacuation of positions. This must be made known to every man in the army. I hold commanding officers responsible for this. The enemy must be made to pave his advance with corpses. The rapid organisation of advanced defensive positions, of intermediate positions behind the principal salients, and positions further in the rear must be carried out by every possible means. The organisations of these latter positions must be begun on the reverse slopes, so that their situation and construction may be hidden from the enemy. I direct that commanding officers shall ensure the maintenance of order behind the line with greatest energy.

Signed v. Below

Extracts from the diary of Richard Brüllka of 6th Coy, 8th Baden Grenadier Regiment

1 July 1916

At about 5 pm alarm. At 6 pm the battalion with first line transport marched away via Bus, Rocquigny to Le Transloy, and bivouacked on the eastern side of the village.

2 July 1916

Battalion is in position. From 9 pm intense gun fire that increases from hour to hour.

4 July 1916

The position of the 3rd Battalion is under heavy fire and the 11th Company is being shot to pieces. Relief is requested. At about 11 o' clock order for stand-by arrives. At 1 o' clock marched away via Grandecourt to Point 110, to collect hand grenades. From there with the commander passing Flers to the middle of Delville Wood, in order to relieve 10th Leib (ie 10th Company).

5 July 1916

In consequence of the commander getting wounded we land in 11th Company's sector and find the trench empty. Owing to a mistake we shall soon become prisoners of the English. Throughout the day continuous gun fire. Towards noon a machine gun brings down an enemy aircraft which plunged on fire in front of our position.

German officers examined a crashed Allied scout plane.

6 July 1916

From 7.30 to 8.30 intense gun fire of all calibres from the English. In spite of great losses the trench is manned immediately after the cessation of fire and the English patrols which were probing, (*und die Fühlenden engl. Patrouillen abgeschmiert*). Everyone awaits the attack but the enemy does not leave his trenches. At once parts of the trench destroyed by shelling is repaired. Losses make it necessary to request reinforcements. In the course of the afternoon our counter barrage paid back the English and the French and put a few obstacles in their way.

Copies of letters to the Western Front

2 July 1916

Grubhoff

... everything is portioned out to us, for each person per month two lbs of sugar. No pork to be had anymore or sausage. The people curse... we have as yet had no distress, but if the war does not end we shall get it badly.

9 July

The bombardment of Bazentin-le-Grand and the trenches held by the regiment was less violent during to-day, and also during to-night than on preceding days. In the course of the afternoon strong English forces advanced from Bernafay Wood and established themselves in Trones Wood until noon. The Reserve Division was to counter-attack at 2 pm in order to recapture the wood. In this the division succeeded during the afternoon. During the night 8/9 July the acting officer, Drexler of the 8th Company, 16th Regiment, succeeded in bringing back to the quarry south of Bazentin-le-Grand two medium trench mortars which the Prussians had abandoned there on 1 July.

(Weather fine)

Losses: altogether 76 killed, 32 wounded.

19 July

This morning strong English forces strenuously attacked Mametz Wood, but were repulsed every time. The machine gun section of the 16th Regiment, which was positioned north-east of Mametz Wood, gave us energetic support in the repelling of these attacks. A patrol of the 7th Company helped in clearing Trones Wood of the English and brought in one officer and a private as prisoners.

Guard Infantry Division – Divisional Order of the Day

8 July 1916

I desire to express my special appreciation of the manner in which the 4th Company, 16th Bavarian Regiment under command of the Reserve Leutnant Rosenthal, surmounted the greatest difficulties

Machine gun teams were most effective in stopping the British attacks.

and courageously brought back into our lines four guns.
(Signed) von Lindequist.

In the course of today very heavy fighting in Mametz Wood, in which No.1 Section of the Machine gun Company, 16th Infantry Regiment, suffered a particularly grievous loss when a single shell fell on a group of men and killed fifteen, plus one platoon commander. Twelve men were wounded. Leutnant Beilhack was this afternoon killed in the trenches near Longueval when he was hit in the head by a shell splinter.

In the afternoon an English aircraft was shot down quite close to Bazentin-le-Grand, about 1,000 metres away. The pilot and observer, two captains, were both brought into the Casualty Clearing Station where I had the opportunity of meeting them.

Towards evening a furious struggle began in Mametz Wood which lasted throughout the night until morning. The III Battalion of the 16th Regiment and the II Battalion of the Lehr Regiment were heavily engaged.

Total losses: 3 killed, 32 wounded, besides Leutnent Beilhack.

Since 2 July I have had a pronounced bronchial cold which does not seem to get any better.

(Weather fine).

Extracts from diaries of prisoners of the 182nd Infantry Regiment (123rd Division) which took part in the fighting in the Bois des Trones and east of Hardecourt.

Remained there until the 17 July under terrible artillery fire. We are living in shell holes. Heavily shelled during and after the relief. Withdrawn to Manancourt and Lieramont where we received our first reinforcements to fill up the gaps. At roll call only 63 of our Company were left.

Paperwork: letters, postcards and diaries all provided information for consideration at British Fourth Army Headquarters. Note the discarded paper on the ground.

On 8 July we arrived on the Somme area. The worst time I have ever had. We were relieved on the 12th but went into the line again on the 13th. Still there throughout the day without hope of relief. We are right in the front line and are suffering heavy losses.

11 July 1916

Berlin

From the 1st August one will not be able to obtain clothing or boots without tickets, and even if one buys things, they are so expensive. Shoes will be up to 40 marks. They already cost 26 marks now. What will they eventually become? There are now two pounds of potatoes every twelve days.

Letter to the Western Front

17 July 1916

Wermsdorf [Saxony]

The hay crop has been delayed owing to the rainy weather. Yesterday our dear father left for the Western Front with a draft for the 183rd Regiment. Now I am left at home alone; unfortunately I didn't see him before he went off. He had to go in such a hurry that I could not even say good-bye. Yes, dear brother, it is hard to have two brothers fighting and then to see one's father go too.

Wermsdorf at the southerly end of the North German Plain of agricultural land set out in crops.

The garrison towns are now being emptied, for the decisive battles now being fought in France – so the papers say. It will mean a lot of young blood being spilt. Father left with a draft of 1,500 men; 500 from Wurzen, 500 from Döbeln and 500 from Leipzig; all old men. At Döbeln, where uncle is, the young fellows start for the front on Thursday and also the fellows from the 1916 Class from Wurzen. We shall soon be called up next.

Here at home things are looking bad as regards food.

German Army Orders of the day by General von Below
Second Army order

3 July 1916

The final outcome of the war depends upon the victory of the Second Army on the Somme. We must win the battle despite the enemy's momentary superiority in guns and infantry.

16 July 1916

His Majesty the Emperor and King in the course of his visit to-day to Army Headquarters has been pleased to express his great satisfaction with the heroic resistance offered by the Second Army to an enemy greatly superior in numbers.

His Majesty is fully convinced that his glorious troops will continue to stand firm and that they will master the enemy's assaults by irresistible dash in the attack, by immovable tenacity in the defence.

Officers and men may be proud of the unshaken confidence placed in them by their Supreme Chief. Let each in his sphere continue to merit that confidence.

The Kaiser boosts morale of his generals by visiting their headquarters on the Somme.

This order will be circulated to all units of the Army.

Signed v. Below

Extract from a letter taken on night 4th/5th

4/5 July 1916

East of Pozières

So the English seem to have advanced a bit. Next few days we had a terrible difficult position. Our regiment's artillery was the only one there and what overpowering odds against us. Our few batteries were always under the fire of from six to ten heavy English batteries. You can imagine our feelings, but not a foot did we retire.

Hostile aircraft – always six to ten in number – above us, flying only 100 metres high – none of our own aircraft in sight. We had no anti-aircraft guns – nothing. It was enough to make one despair. Naturally, they discovered all our positions and this explains why we were so accurately shelled so often. Every calibre of gun to the very largest laid down fire on our positions. Aeroplanes!

War diary, Leutnant Oberst Bedall

11 July 1916

During the day very heavy and methodical shelling of the Regimental sector from 9 am till late evening by big guns of heavy calibre, including 28 cm. Bazentin-le-Grand suffered terribly but the sector held by the III Battalion of the Lehr Regiment suffered no less on our immediate right.

Bazentin-le-Grand is to-day a scene of war and devastation which cannot be improved upon. In the evening between 9 and 10 o'clock the enemy bombarded Bazentin village with gas shells, without however, doing serious damage. Otherwise somewhat quieter. A list of casualties sustained by the III Battalion of the 16th Regiment, which found the situation inside Mametz Wood to be very unfavourable and suffered severely in consequence shows:

1. Oberleutnant of Reserve Reinhold killed by rifle bullet
2. Leutnant of Reserve Wagner slightly wounded
3. Leutnant of Reserve Schneider slightly wounded
4. Leutnant of Reserve Weinberger seriously wounded
5. Hauptmann Woller slightly wounded
6. Leutnant Francip seriously wounded
7. Leutnant Vogt slightly wounded
8. Leutnant Mans seriously wounded
9. Ensign Trollsch slightly wounded

Losses: 13 killed, 54 wounded and 11 missing.

Extract from a letter from Stuttgart

31 July 1916

There are now cards for cloth and suits of clothing, but these things are only obtainable if one really need the things. Only expensive types of cloth can be bought without cards.

31 July 1916

We had an awful scare a week ago last Saturday, aeroplanes were sighted near here, they however, did not reach Stuttgart.

Men of the III Battalion Württemberg 127th Infantry Regiment, 26th Division at Ulm railway station on their way to the front.

Extracts from the diary of an officer of the 127th Infantry Regiment, XIII Corps. Left the Ypres front 29th July for the Somme.

Written upon arrival on the Somme front:

30 July 1916

What we hear is incredible. The troops here have only one front line position, instead of a second and third line as we are used to. On the other hand the transport wagons are protected by concrete, but not ready to move; some of them had broken axles, wheels etc. The experiences of the Champagne battle had not been taken advantage of in any way. This was the reason we had so much transport was lost. Further the transport park was not protected, so that enemy

aircraft were able to cause enormous losses from low altitude attacks. Our airmen are rabbits; not one shows himself over the lines.

Extracts from a letter found on the body of Landsturm Silberman, 119th Grenadier Regiment, 26th Division

31 July 1916

Nurnberg

Dear Max,

To-day we received your letter, how you will be in that hell on the Somme. The enemy are claiming that your regiment lost 2,000 men – our Army Command states 500. What is it really? Are the enemy right, then please answer 'yes', if not write 'no'. I know of a Bavarian regiment that lost 1,900 men and all its officers except two; a leutnant took command of the regiment.

Letter to a man in the 125th Infantry Regiment, 26th Division

16 July 1916

Tübingen

This morning at 9 o'clock I went to the Goods Station to see how they detrain the wounded, for twenty-two coaches arrived again, mostly with seriously wounded cases on board, many without legs or arms.

Letter written in shorthand by a German soldier (Unit unknown)

Since the beginning of July an unparalleled slaughter has been taking place. Not a day passes but the English let their gas waves off towards our trenches, at one point or another. I'll give you just one instance of the effects of this gas. People seven to eight kilometres behind the front line have become unconscious from the remnants of the gas cloud. Its effects are felt even twelve kilometres behind the front. One has only to look at the rifles after a gas attack to see what deadly stuff it is. They are red with rust as if they had lain out for weeks in the mud. Also the effect of the continuous bombardment is indescribable.

British report on the effects of a 15-inch shell

11 July 1916

When our troops entered Contalmaison it was found that a British 15 inch shell had landed in the château and penetrated to the cellar; 95 dead Germans were discovered here.

Noteable prisoners

Among the prisoners taken is the chef of the Cafe Royal, London. He is reported wounded.

A prisoner stated that the Germans shoot prisoners they capture upon whom any German letters of buttons are found. Spies: a prisoner recently stated that he believed German aviators dropped men behind our lines and picked them up some three days afterwards. Possibly the pigeons which have been seen several times flying from our lines over to the Germans may have connections with these spies.

Information given by Hermann Lohrmann 2 Company, 51st Reserve Regiment, 12th Reserve Division

Before the war worked with an English firm in Belgium. (William Fowler, steam engine manufacturer). He returned to Germany on the outbreak of war; not called up until 21 September 1915 on account of his having a broken arm. He trained at Ralibor remained there doing a blacksmith's work. While at Ralibor he was called in to mend a lamp which hung over a table of his Brigade Commander, who was temporarily in command of the division. When taking the lamp from the office, he saw on the table a secret document from the German War Office in reply to a letter from the Divisional Commander asking whether it was necessary to send to the front men with only two fingers or one eye. This letter stated that since the war had begun the Germans had 2,750,000 men permanently unfit for service and 1,933,000 killed.

From a letter written by an officer to 22nd Reserve Field Artillery Regiment but never posted

7th July 1916

We were in the second line for some days. Tonight we go forward for two days. Much is required from us here more than before Verdun, for we are very short of artillery and aircraft.

The edge of Mametz Wood with wrecked German artillery wagons littering the roadside.

Officer captured in Mametz Wood, early morning

10 July 1916

The officer captured was a company commander and was very downhearted. He had been greatly impressed by the artillery fire and he said he did not consider the slaughter of his infantry by concentrated artillery fire as fair war, but a device for slaughtering men.

XV Corps 10 July 1916.

Joseph Brizintzy, 3rd Company, 51st Reserve Regiment caught Trones Wood

7 July 1916

The morale is pretty good, but naturally after two years of war they do not fight with the same keenness as they did in the beginning. The general opinion of the Prussian Guards is that they are only the 'elite' and do not 'stick it'. Shelling here has been very bad, worse than that at Verdun.

The following is a translation of a German document found in a dug out near La Boisselle

Expressions to be learned by heart

When Englishmen are met in the trenches shout out:

'Hands up you fool!' to be pronounced – *Honds opp ju fuhl.*

'Arms away!' *Arms ewa.*

At the entrance of a dugout shout: Is anybody inside?'

Is anibodi inseid.

After throwing in a hand grenade shout out: 'Come all out, quick, quick.' *Kom ohl aut, quick, quick.*

If the Englishmen come out shout at them: 'Hands up come on Tommy!' *Honds opp kom on Tomy.*

If the fellows want hurrying cry out: 'Go on. Go on'.

Extract from a German letter written in the trenches

9 July 1916

Today I am spending my first Sunday in the trenches but in dreadful anxiety as our lives are in danger every minute. Grenade after grenade explodes over and in front of us. I shall be glad when we are relieved as I have become so nervous that I tremble like a dog. Add to this the bad weather for we are standing up to our knees in water. The English throw as many grenades as we do shells. They do not all hit but they come like rain... I could tell you many

All the comforts of home for these German soldiers safe in their deep, well constructed shelters. Wherever and whenever these positions were captured, paperwork, in the form of orders, diaries and letters from home, were collected for translation by British Intelligence.

experiences and I have already had enough of the war... Here I sit in a hole which I have made to get a bit of shelter and write to you dear wife. If you were to see me you would not recognise me – dirt from head to foot. I wish I could be made a prisoner as then I would not have to endure this misery anymore for I cannot stand it much longer.

British VIII Corps

The Regimental Commander and Staff of the 18th Bavarian Infantry Regiment were captured this morning in Bazentin-le-Petit

The Regimental Commander and Staff of the Lehr Regiment were captured by the Corps on our left.

11 July 1916

Prisoners report, 3rd Battalion, 51st Reserve Infantry Regiment, 12 Reserve Division, VI Reserve Corps, captured in Trones Wood. There is a Corps order that Trones Wood must be held at any price and a prisoner thinks that the Germans will not spare any sacrifice to hold it. The directive is: 'To the last man'.

Report of a prisoner belonging to the Sanitäts Section captured in Mametz Wood

12 July 1916

Prisoner describes German losses as very heavy – four divisions being practically out of action. Prisoner named 183rd, 185th and 3rd Guards divisions, and says 190th Infantry Regiment suffered especially heavy. Of many companies only five to twenty men could be mustered. He describes confusion behind the lines as very bad. He states that a number of men from various companies and regiments are gathered from stragglers in the rear and pushed into the fight. He says that he has heard that many officers have been shot by their own men.

14 July 1916

Three German field guns and two 8-inch howitzers were captured yesterday near Bazentin-le-Grand by the Corps on our left.

13 July 1916

Another public character has just fallen into our hands (amongst a number of other prisoners) in the person of the former Head Waiter of the Carlton Hotel, London.

Bucharest 11 July 1916

Bulgarian deserters who have arrived at Turtukai relate that the 16th Bulgarian Infantry Regiment has mutinied and killed its German officers, while the regiment sent to punish the mutineers joined hands with them. Many Austrians have deserted from the monitors on the Danube and taken refuge on Romanian territory. At the present time there are 9,000 Bulgarian and Austro-Hungarian deserters interned in concentration camps in Romania.

Talismans

A number of curious talismans have been found on prisoners and enemy dead designed to render them immune from death, wounds or capture, and such like calamities. For the most part they are a mix of prayers, curses, and apparently meaningless phrases in a strange and incoherent jumble. Unfortunately it is impossible in the nature of things to procure specimens of an effective type. Those procured are presumable defective in some important particular – and failed their unfortunate owners when actually put to the test. The following 'horoscope' was found on a post card taken from a prisoner secured by the VIII Corps, shows to what straits the enemy is reduced to bolster up his flagging spirits.

The Horoscope of Peace

	Kaiser Wilhelm	Kaiser Franz Joseph
Geboren (born)	1859	1830
Alter (age)	57	86
Anfang der Regierung (beginning of reign)	1888	1858
Dauer (length of it)	28	58
	3832	3832

Half of it = 1916; then two full stops = 1.9.16
War will end 1st September 1916.

A Württemberg infantryman in full equipment which includes a trench flashlight.

Contents of a diary

From a diary amongst the documents captured by VIII Corps it appears that the writer was now and again detailed for patrol and said 'duty'. He outlines the bracketed comment 'not voluntary'. At other time he appears to have been detailed for the deep digging of abandoned gardens under oversight of an officer. The entries 'In one garden we found cognac and wine' and again, 'we found from sixty to seventy bottles of wine in one garden' supply the motive for this activity.

Captured German order

9 July 1916

Regimental order read out to 5 Company of Reserve Infantry Regiment No.122.

I intend to strengthen the battalions by the incorporation of drafts from the recruit depôt. Detailed returns of the fighting strength of the battalions and their ration requirements must therefore be submitted without delay on the usual form.

I express my heartiest thanks to the officers in the front line for the splendid manner in which they have in every way kept me abreast of developments by their reports. Thanks to the gods the regiment so far has been spared all surprises. Also I must thank the men for their exemplary conduct during the strenuous days we have of late passed through. Nothing has affected that, not even the regrettable way in which the 2nd Battalion has been imperilled by the fire of our own artillery. This incident has been made by me the subject of a rigorous and strict enquiry. Especially the resulting loss of the lives of faithful comrades.

God grant that the offensive power of our greatest enemies in this war may also in the future be stayed by our resistance.

Signed Kumml

Translation of a letter

Written by a man of the 1st Battalion 106th Reserve Infantry Regiment.

10 July 1918

We are at present near Peronne. Yesterday the French and British attacked ten times. Here the artillery fire is terrible; all the world has not witnessed such a fire before. To-night we are going in the front line, there are no trenches now; we all lay in the open field. Of the 23rd Regiment only 100 men out of a thousand returned. We have terrible losses and no one can bring us rations.

Good wishes for the present, Paul.

I have given our Sergeant Major 50 Marks.

Morale

The prisoners of the 16th Bavarian Regiment said that they did not care to fight side by side with the Prussians. The morale of the Lehr Regiment does not appear to be good. Some prisoners said that they were commanded by insolent young officers.

The chief reasons given by the prisoners for their defeat:

1. Our artillery, especially heavy guns
2. Exhaustion of their supply of hand-grenades
3. Chaos in the distribution of units along the front
4. Lack of water

Letter to Frau M.B.

Munich

From her brother 6th Company, 16 Regiment, 10th Bavarian Infantry Division.

13 July 1916

My dear sister Marie,

Only a few lines in haste to inform you that I have received yours as well as Maria's card which gave me immense pleasure. As I have already told you my Regiment has been transferred to the Somme region. We are since 1st in an un-entrenched position in a region where the English lads seem in fact to play the game properly. Our trenches have been completely overrun, and what we have gone through since this time and suffered under the English artillery fire can scarcely be described here. It put the greatest strain on the physical strength and endurance of our troops and one asks oneself if it is possible for men to hold up under such things. The village where we are, which is close to a well known wood, is now only a

German sentry protects himself against British gas.

heap of ruins and offers a spectacle of the uttermost desolation.

Today I experienced for the first time a sample of a gas shell. That is the worst means of fighting which one can think up. I was just helping to get comrades out of a dug-out where the shell had burst when suddenly, I myself went quite queer in the head, and lost all notion of what was passing around me. I was just strong enough to pull myself out of the hole and was able to lower myself down onto a pile of chalk in the open. After some time I recovered. But two of my comrades became very afraid and stared wildly around them like idiots without recognising anyone. They were convinced that someone was tearing their lungs to pieces. We could only stand and look on unable to help them – they were unable to help themselves and wept like little children. After an hour it had passed and they began to recover but were unable to speak. What are shell and shrapnel compared to this?

We will probably be relieved tomorrow or the day after. The weather remains fine. We all look like wild animals.

Unposted letter

Written by a man of the 190th Regiment, 185th Division. This division reached the Somme area from Champagne on the night of 2nd/3rd July 1916.

11 July 1916

Gueudecourt

To the front and back again: always backwards and forwards. Yesterday we marched from Beaumetz to Velu; the day before yesterday, from Martinpuich to Beaumetz; today from Velu to this place. Camping in the open all the time with no sleep and with feet burning so that we can hardly stand up. The whole of the 1st Battalion, 190th Regiment, had scarcely 120 of its 1,100 men left. The 3rd and 2nd Battalions each lost more than half. Now once again we are directly behind the lines, this village being shelled on and off. There is no thought of leave at present. I hope that this awful business will soon stop; it is dreadful here.

German Emperor on the Somme Sector

From an article in the German press dated 17 July 1916, it appears that the German Emperor was present in the Somme area on the 16 July. After receiving a report on the operations from the army commanders and holding a consultation with the Chief of the General Staff, General Falkenhayn, the Emperor visited some of the Field Hospitals, where he distributed Iron Crosses to the wounded and praised the bravery of his troops.

Enemy losses

A captured diary belonging to a German Commanding Officer shows that in the fighting on 1 July, the 6th Bavarian Reserve Regiment, which opposed us at Montauban suffered 3,000 casualties out of a total strength of 3,500 men. Another document shows that one battalion of the 190th Regiment lost 980 men out of 1,100, while the other two battalions of that regiment each lost more that half of their effective strength.

Chief of the General Staff, General Falkenhayn.

Captured Documents

Message from 3rd Battalion, 16th Bavarian Infantry Regiment, to the Lehr Regiment.

11 July 1916

2 pm Battalion partly non existent. Could not stand the fire of the heavy howitzer battery, which for several hours has systematically and successfully bombarded the dug-outs of the second line. Could these guns be subdued by our own artillery?

As regards the condition of the 3rd Battalion of the 16th Bavarian Infantry Regiment. I regard it as my duty to point out that the men remaining are severely shaken, so that their fighting value is to be rated very low. The heavy fire; the impression made on the men by the wounded and the dead; the difficulty of bringing up food, and its frequent absence, are the cause. From the front line I have had no report up till now.

Signed von Reitz, Major

Commanding 3rd Battalion, 16 Bavarian Infantry Regiment

Unposted letter

Written by a man of the 190th Infantry Regiment, 185th Division.

13 July 1916

Our Company Commander, our Captain and nearly all the officers and corporals are either wounded or dead. Only about forty-five to fifty men of our Company are left. I was a most terrible fight and I went through the whole of it. Everyone had to join in even the carpenter, shoe makers, the tailor and the orderlies. This place is called La Boisselle, near Albert, about twenty kilometres from Arras, where we came to grips with the English. You could never believe the terrible artillery bombardment we have had to live through, but we are managing to keep them back. Our Battalion has been in the thick of it for four days and nights. We had to remain in

Letters home and playing a game of cards. It was captured letters to and from the homeland that provided the British with some indication of how their efforts were affecting the enemy.

the trenches with water and mud up to our knees until we were relieved by another Brigade.

I should like to tell you of one thing which is really too terrible, and that is our officers have to drive us into the fight with drawn revolvers.

Were it not for the fact that I had both you dear people to think of I should wish that I might be released of all these terrible happenings.

Captured German documents

Copy of a German document found among the papers taken from the Headquarters of the 3rd Battalion, 10th Reserve Infantry Regiment, 28th Reserve Division.

XIV Reserve Korps
General Command
Ia 1279
Notice for each dug-out in the front position

1. Our infantry is superior to any enemy, they either resist to the utmost or die.

2. Our dug-outs are proof against the heaviest and longest artillery bombardments. They must leave them at the correct time however, when the enemy attack arrives and hurry to the fire-step. Anyone remaining in them will be in danger of being killed by hand-grenades, or rendered unconscious by gas. Therefore, get out!

3. Rifles and hand-grenades are not to be stored in the entrances to dug-outs. They might easily get buried there. Therefore take them down into the dug-out with you. Also the machine guns.

4. Don't fear a gas attack, even when it blackens the air. The gas soon wafts behind. Put on protectors, place wooden boxes before you and set them alight. Only those troops who lose their heads during a gas attack have been beaten by the enemy. The steadfast troops have repulsed attacks.

5. Don't use the rifle until you are at the breastwork, nor the hand-grenades until the enemy is near. They are often thrown too early.

I. If the enemy gets into the trenches, continue to fight with hand-grenades. Help will come at once from behind and from the flanks. Everyone in the neighbouring trenches must also stand to if the enemy enter there.

II. If the enemy break through don't lose your head! Only weak-kneed troops surrender. Brave troops continue fighting rearguard

Maschinengewehr wird in Stellung gebracht; links der Gewehrschrank.

This German postcard depicts rifles being stored in a cabinet in the front line trench, a practice that would be forbidden during the Somme battles 'Rifles and hand-grenades are not to be stored in the entrances to dug-outs'. The text reads: Machine gun is placed in position on the left of the gun cabinet.

actions. In this way brave troops have taken thousands of prisoners in recent battles.

III. Rations and drinkables will always be supplied to the troops even during battles lasting several days.

The Commanding General, (Sd) von Stein.

Bringing in German wounded.

Examination of wounded prisoners

Men of the 8th Bavarian Reserve Regiment, 10 Bavarian Division, captured north of Ovillers.

17 July 1916

Training: After four weeks training, they were marched to various villages for further exercises and then went to Villers-Guislain, where they remained fourteen days.

On 10 July 1916, 300 men (mixed ex-wounded and Landsturm of all ages and nationalities) came up from Zweibrucken. These were attached to interrogated man's draft of 100. The 200 men of 6th Bavarian Reserve Regiment and 16th Bavarian Regiment were left in Villers-Guislain. The now draft of around 400 strong were then taken in motor lorries via Bapaume to Warlencourt. From there they marched to Courcelette. At Courcelette they were divided into Companies for the 8th Bavarian Reserve Regiment: 200 for the 9th Company; 200 for the 4th Company. The draft then marched for the front from Courcelette and came under heavy artillery fire and suffered heavy losses. Men became demoralised; some got into nearby dug-outs; others including NCOs and officers ran away and everything became confused. Oberleutnant Brachtel of the 22nd Bavarian Regiment collected the remainder and pushed them up to reinforce the Guard Fusileer Regiment in Ovillers. The interrogated prisoner describes the state of affairs as chaotic in the 6th Company, 3rd Battalion, Guard Fusileer Regiment. The N.C.O.s with revolvers kept the men to their posts but did not advance themselves.

Food was obtained from Courcelette and Mouquet Farm but water was scarce and food bad. There is a spring at Mouquet Farm. The prisoner was wounded 16 July.

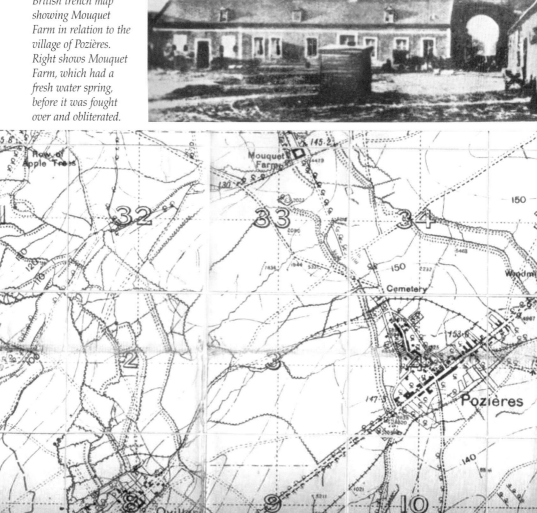

British trench map showing Mouquet Farm in relation to the village of Pozières. Right shows Mouquet Farm, which had a fresh water spring, before it was fought over and obliterated.

Extract from a letter written to a German soldier by a male friend

23 July 1916

Here we are doing very badly in the way of food. Last week's menu card:

Day	Breakfast	Mid-day	Afternoon	Supper
Monday	1 slice of bread	Maggi soup Pudding bread	Nothing	Bread
Tuesday	2 slices of bread	Soup - 1 egg and bread	Nothing	Bread
Wednesday	2 slices of bread	Bean soup without bacon	Nothing	Bread
Thursday	2 slices of bread	Nothing at all!	Bread	Bread
Friday	2 slices of bread & butter	Soup, $1^1/2$ ozs meat. Pudding	Nothing	Bread
Saturday	2 slices of bread	Pea soup	Nothing	Bread
Sunday	2 slices of bread	$1^1/2$ ozs meat, 4 potatoes, veg Cake	Bread	Bread

Isn't that splendid?

There is still enough to go round however. If one wants to really get something into his stomach one has to keep on drinking hard. At Bishofs I always drink from one of the big pots, of course they cost $2^1/2$d, but there is more in them.

Examination of Commanders of 3rd Battalion, 62nd Regiment and 2nd Battalion, 27th Regiment

The Battalion Commander of the 3rd Battalion, 62nd Regiment captured 23 July 1916, stated that he had entirely lost touch with units on either side. On his right, a part of a battalion of the 157th Infantry

Regiment was to come under his command, and on his left lay, he thought, another battalion of his own regiment. He did not succeed at any time in establishing touch, through, as he stated, lack of orderlies. Prisoner confessed that these were very critical days, but was confident that Germany had sufficient forces to continue to stem the continued assaults of the Allies on the western and Eastern fronts, until these died away in consequence of the losses always sustained by the attacking forces. Prisoner knew Major Moraht of the *Berliner Tageblat* personally and thought that he was a good writer on the military situation and knew what he was talking about. His views were generally very sound as his writing was objective and impersonal.

Prisoner expressed great admiration for our infantry. The Battalion Commander of the 2nd Battalion, 27th Regiment, who was captured yesterday morning, commented on the speed with which our machine-gun sections brought weapons into action, and on the good distribution of their fire. No sooner was ground gained than effective machine-gun fire swept the new field of fire and established a barrage at points of tactical importance. Our successes as so far gained are attributed in large measure to the skill and daring of the British airmen in depriving the enemy of all means of aerial observation. It is stated that the German Flying Corps have lost heavily in prestige as a result of recent operations.

German casualties – Verdun

An analysis of the official German list of casualties sustained at Verdun shows that the killed, wounded and missing in infantry regiments were in the following proportion:

Of total casualties:

Killed	23%
Missing	7%
Wounded	70%

The casualties among officers amount to 31% of their establishment; those of the men to 49%.

The proportion of officer casualties to men was 1 to 52. The proportion of officer casualties to men on establishment is 1 to 33.

Examination of Leutnant Hase

Machine Gun Company, 2nd Battalion, Lehr Regiment 8.

The Machine Company came up five days ago from Transloy, where it had been resting, and relieved the Machine Gun Company of the

12th Regiment. The prisoner was taken at map reference 5. 18a. 6.4, where his machine gun had been in position. It was knocked out by a direct hit by our artillery and the prisoner himself was sheltering in a dug-out, where he was surrounded on all sides and captured. The German officers interviewed expressed great admiration at the daring of our Flying Corps and were surprised at the exactness of our trench maps.

They considered that the fighting here was more severe than at Verdun. Leutnant Hase stated that the attack on the Great Fortress of Verdun was a great mistake on the part of their General Staff, and seemed to think that if the attack had been directed against some other part of the line the Germans would have broken through.

They seemed to think that the Flers line, which they described as very strong, would hold up the British advance.

Much heavy artillery has arrived in the last few days and none of it has come from Verdun.

Extract from War Diary No.4

Leutnant-Oberst Bedall, Officer Commanding 16th Bavarian Infantry Regiment.

The necessary artillery and infantry reinforcements were to some extent concentrated towards the end of June. From this we deduced that very difficult times awaited us.

The position became critical when it transpired that the 6th Bavarian Reserve Regiment, which on the morning of 1 July was thrown into the fighting around Montauban, had been completely destroyed. Of 3,000 men only 500 survivors remain, and these are for the most part men who had not taken part in the battle; plus two regimental officers plus a few stragglers who turned up on the following day. All the rest are dead, wounded or missing. Only a small fraction fell into the enemy's hands as prisoners. The Regimental Staff and the Battalion Staffs, have all been captured in their dug-outs. The 6th Bavarian Reserve Regiment is said to have surrendered owing to the complete shortage of ammunition, which had all been expended, but they maintained an heroic resistance until the last moment.

These dirty English are said to have slain these brave people without mercy despite that fact that the lack of ammunition rendered them all but defenceless, although by signals they indicated their readiness to surrender.

Letters from Berlin to a fusileer

11 July 1916

Dear Friend,

Up to now I am happy to say that I have not been conscripted, but it cannot last much longer. The Past alone has sent 3,000 men. So what do you think? I believe that it will all come to an end soon as things seem very bad here. This week we get 2 lbs of potatoes per head. Well Albert I have received all you sent and thank you very much. Many greetings from your friend Erich.

9 July 1916

From his sister:

Dear Albert,

On the 4th we sent you cigarettes and chocolate. Here in Berlin one has already to starve. In eight days only 2 lbs of potatoes. Enough for one mouthful eh? Here everyone hopes for peace this year. On Fohren Island, Schleswick Holstein, is a poplar tree which has not bloomed for forty-six years, but is in bloom again now. The Fohreners are saying therefore, that peace will come again this year. It was so in 1871. This is in the papers.

Mobile soup kitchen on the streets of Berlin in 1916.

Examination of an NCO of the 10th Company, 3rd Battalion, 38 Reserve Infantry Regiment

30 July 1916

Captured in the sunken road south-west of Guillemont (T.30. bd). He said that his company came into position through Wedge Wood to the south-east corner of Guillemont (T25. b17) and hence across country into the sunken road. They lost thirty men from shell fire before reaching the trench, including ten who were knocked out by a direct hit. They arrived in line on the night of 28 July and lost about 50% killed and wounded in the two days 28 to 30 July. Our artillery fire, he said, was very heavy and accurate. There were practically no 'duds'. They were very short of water, having only what was in their water bottles. No field cookers could be brought up owing to the barrage and they lived on iron rations. Their morale, he said, was poor. Our artillery fire had so demoralised the men that they did not care what happened. Company strength in the trenches was 120 men as a company remained behind.

His company composition: 7% Active, 43% Landstrum, 44% Landwehr, 6% Recruits 1915/16 class.

Leutnant Oberst Bedall's war diary (continued)

1 to 3 July 1916
Losses:

Officers	Killed	Wounded	Sick
I BATT	1	1	2
II BATT	-	-	-
III BATT	1	-	-
MG MS 44	-	1	-
MG Coy	-	1	-
MG MS 87	-	-	-

NCOs/Men	Killed	Wounded	Sick
I BATT	14	26	44
II BATT	25	47	58
III BATT	7	7	21

Total			
Officers	2	2	-
Rank & File	46	80	123

Missing 50
Sick 2 officers 15 men

*The centre of the
village of
Guillemont after it
was captured by
the British.*

**Extracts from a conversation with the officer commanding
4th Company, 1st Battalion, 75th Reserve Infantry Regiment**

30/31 July 1916

Captured in S.2.d. Intermediate line.

This officer was wounded by a grenade in the Intermediate line. He
stated that the line was held by three companies (1st Batt, 75 RIR) with
a large proportion of machine guns. At the time of our assault. The
prisoner's company was the centre of the three companies and held
the sector from S.2.d 4.6 to S.2.d. 95 55.

Instructions had been given to this officer by his commander that a
British attack was to be expected any time. His orders were to 'hold on
as long as possible, but not at all costs'. He was told that he would
have plenty of time to man the parapet and put his machine guns into
position before the time came when our final barrage lifted and the
appearance of the assaulting British infantry. The prisoner, (who
claims that he has fought in several different sectors of the British front
on occasions when we have assaulted) stated that our infantry
attacked with great dash and determination and that they moved
across the open to the assault so close up under our artillery barrage

that as the artillery lifted the infantry were on top of the enemy parapet and this gave the Germans no time to man the trenches and place their machine guns in position.

He states the attack was carried out in this manner especially well opposite the sector and left of his front. But he was of the opinion that the British troops that attacked the right of the intermediate line were slower in the assault and did not go forward under the barrage so well as the other assaulting troops, as he knew that company on his right had not been broken in upon like his.

Kirchbach's Group, Corps HQ

30 July 1916

I have assumed command of what was known as Gossler's Group. I have complete confidence that each man placed under my orders – Prussians, Bavarians, Württembergers and Saxons – will realise the greatness of of the obligations placed on him and that he will do his duty to his last breath.
Signed von Kirchbach.

Extracts from a German War Diary

27 July 1916

I request that drafts be carefully instructed in the use of hand grenades in order to avoid the continual occurrence of accidents.
(Signed) Wischer

Extract from a letter taken from a German prisoner

30 July 1916

Zuriesel

Shortly there will be no more meat, no fat, no butter. Eggs can't be had anymore. Yesterday I went to queue at the butchers; at 8 pm there was no more pork to be had and I couldn't get any anywhere else. It is terrible how the women fight and must fight to get anything at all. It is the same with everything. There is very little flour to be obtained. Rose must cook with Hungarian black flour. It is really only fodder. One cannot even think of macaroni let alone getting any to eat. For everything one needs coupons. After August we shall be issued with clothing coupons as well.

Right: Queueing for potatoes.

Below: Berlin housewives queueing outside a general store for butter.

The following translation of captured documents throw fresh light on the German High Command in the Somme area:

30 July 1916

Gallwitz Army Group (Heeresgruppe)

My Order of the Day.

In the coming days we must be prepared for an all-out assault by the enemy. The decisive battle of the war is now being fought on the fields of the Somme. It must be impressed on every officer and man right up to the front line that the fate of our country is at stake in this struggle. By ceaseless vigilance and self-sacrificing courage the enemy must be prevented from gaining another inch of ground. His attacks must break up against a solid wall of German breasts.

The Commander-in-Chief (*Obersbefehlshaber*)

Signed von Gallitz, General of Artillerie.

A captured Russian Maxim machine gun in place on the Somme front to help break up the British attacks.

Chapter Three

Fighting in August 1916

Captured German Order
Army Group Gallwitz, Artillery Staff, HQ – SECRET

1 August 1916

105 mm gun. The order from General Max Gallwitz directed that a gun was to be kept in reserve so that in times of heavy usage there could be an exchange of pieces and time given for the breech and barrel to cool down.

My attention is called to the incredibly high number of cases of cracked barrels of field guns, apparently due to careless handling. If an improvement does not take place the supply will be unable to keep pace with requirements. This will result in a diminishing in the power of our artillery. Study carefully the War Office Notice 2400/6/16 a. 4. regarding field artillery munitions and their use.

Cracked barrels are usually the result of clumsy handling, dirty ammunition, or soil on heated barrels. Again attention is called to the advisability in rapid fire of keeping one out of

General Max Gallwitz.

The results when a shell exploded upon leaving the the breech. This 105 mm gun has blown apart directly behind the trunnion

action so that it may be examined and cleaned. If guns are duly changed then over heating will be avoided.

Signed von Gallwitz

Letter found on a prisoner belonging to the 84th Regiment 5 August 1916

Captured at Pozières

I cannot tell you more – only the news about Pozières fighting can be summed up in a word, for in truth the state of affairs here resembles nothing else on earth. Heaps of corpses, a horrible stench and among the wire entanglements pieces of dead men. The 84th Regiment has lost at least two thirds of its strength. No time for more. We are at present 600 yards behind, but tomorrow it's back again to the front line. It is simply desperate. For heaven's sake send a parcel of food. One has nothing to eat and there is nothing to drink.

Extracts from a conversation with German officers from 84th Reserve Infantry Regiment and 162nd Infantry Regiment

4/5 August 1916

Captured during the night.

They claimed that it was dangerous to show themselves in the German trenches, even around the entrances to their dug-outs when a

The trenches and dugouts after the Germans had been driven out of the remains of the village of Pozières following the attacks of 29 July and 4 August by the Australians and Canadians.

British aeroplane was above. They believed that British aircraft signalled the position of any men they saw back to gun batteries, leading to fire being brought down on those points. All officers said that they knew that an attack must be coming, but they did not know when. Our artillery puzzled them by bombarding them at various times during the nights. No attacks followed these bombardments, although at first they half expected it. They were not expecting an attack after our final bombardment. They had been convinced that if made at any time then it would be dawn. Many of the machine guns had been buried in the dug-outs by this bombardment.

The company of the officer of 162nd Infantry Regiment had lost eighty-four men in four days during the bombardment, The regiment was set to be relieved the next morning by 84th Reserve Infantry Regiment. They had plenty to eat and drink. Reliefs and reinforcements at any rate during action used to be brought in into O.G.2, over the top and not through communication trenches. The position of O.G.2, immediately south of the Bapaume Road was too much battered to hold. They could only crawl about in this part. One officer was surprised to find that we regarded it as occupied. The Windmill had been used as an observation post, but it had been so battered by our artillery that it had not lately been in use.

The attack was unexpected. Our men were on the enemy very quickly, especially just south of the Bapaume Road. An officer in Tour Trench found himself cut off by our troops getting into his trench, beyond him, as well as either side of him.

An officer of the 84th Regiment said that at about 10.30 he was marching into the trench near the windmill at the head of about fifty men when our bombardment opened up suddenly on them. In O.G.2 the first thing he found was three wounded Australians. He judged that the British must be making an attack and ordered his men to form to the right and counter-attack. In forming the right lost touch with him going, he thought, too far to the north. He found himself alone with just three men. They went over O.G.2 and dug in in a crater between it and O.G.1. There they were surrounded and captured.

The first question which the officer of the 162nd Regiment asked when he reached our Brigade HQ was, 'Are you in Courcelette?' He was told 'No, but your batteries have been seen blowing up their ammunition.' At once he asked, 'Were they heavy batteries or light ones?'

One officer of the 84th Regiment said that he thought neither side would win the war, 'nobody will win it'. He thought that it would end

Captured German officers – a potential source of important information – if one could be encouraged to talk.

in September. Another said that Germany would fight on until she could get a satisfactory peace.

They had been informed that immediately after the Jutland Sea Battle the British recalled all their large cruisers from colonies and elsewhere overseas.

One prisoner stated that the men were very much afraid of our grenades as their effect is very powerful and our men throw them a great distance. They had numerous casualties from them. Their morale is good and they are confident of winning the war.

Interrogation of a leutnant of the 9th Company, 3rd Battalion, 127th Infantry Regiment, 27th Division

7 August 1916

Captured about 2.30 am south-east of Arrow Head Copse, whilst endeavouring to get in touch with the left of the 120th Regiment which is positioned about 5.30 8080. He stated that the Germans main Second line trench from south of Guillemont to Wedge Wood is unoccupied. It is entirely smashed by artillery fire.

They get no ordinary water in the line. There is a well in Combles, but it is marked 'undrinkable'. A bottle of soda water is brought up nightly for every man, also wine for officers and men. They have no water carts or means of sterilising wells.

Leutnant-Oberst Bedall, officer commanding 16th Bavarian Infantry Regiment

War diary (continued)

The regimental staff had moved its battle headquarters from Longueval to Bazentin-le-Grand. In the last named place was also the Staff of the 26th Reserve Brigade (Major-General von Dressler and Hauptmann of Artillery, von Bredon). The 16th Regiment was under the command of this brigade. It had thus moved into the dug-out of the Brigade Staff. A heavy battle raged all day; villages, roads, trenches and troops came under an intense artillery fire. Even the Regimental staff could with difficulty only reach its new battle headquarters after it had left Longueval, for that too was now exposed to heavy shelling. The I Battalion succeeded in retiring to its allotted position with relatively small losses, because use was made of the dead ground east of the small road, Mametz Wood to Bazentin-le-Grand. But the II Battalion was forced to remain in the quarry and immediately west of it until midnight, and was all the time exposed to shell fire and to very heavy machine-gun fire. Finally it succeeded in reaching its position in the sector Bazentin-le-Grand – Longueval and establishing itself there. The retirement towards the morning was effected by splitting up into small groups. The days 1st and 2nd July were very hard for the 16th Bavarians and it suffered heavy loss. But the men carried out their

A Bavarian infantryman of a type Leutnant Oberst (Lt. Colonel) Bedall was proud to command.

duties bravely caring little for death or wounds and thereby maintained its reputation of the 16th Bavarians and as heroes.

I greatly rejoice over the achievements of the Regiment, which met with unstinted praise of all our superiors. I am proud to command such a fine regiment.

Quotation from the *Molnische Volkszeitung* (peoples' daily newspaper)

We have suffered heavy losses in human lives and in human happiness and now the question is, 'What is going to happen next?' No one can say when there will be peace. There is no sign that our enemies have given up their idea of annihilating us. We continue to fight for our existence and we are all struggling for a peace that will guarantee as against another world war. We know that there is no war in which there are neither victors nor vanquished. In this war also there will be a victor and those conquered. If we are not the conquerors we shall be the conquered and shall have to suffer the consequences. Even if we declared that we were ready to conclude a peace without victors and vanquished, our enemies would, without exception, laugh in our face. Therefore there is only one order possible: 'Hold out!'

Extract of a letter to a man in 4th Company, 361st Regiment

5th August

Berlin

However did you get into the 361st? You are lucky as the 27th had some heavy losses on the Somme. The 1917 are already at the front in Russia.

German letter from Mittenwald

23 August 1916

Munich 17 June 1916

In Munich things went very bad last Saturday. The poor women were having to stand throughout the nights in order to get meat the following morning. In the 'Free Bank' they get no bread or butter cards and without tickets you can get nothing. Then a beast of a Prussian (he must have been an officer) said that they ought to drive their children to pasture so that they could eat grass. Then the storm broke loose and they had to bring the soldiers out. However, they sided with the poor people. Then came the mounted police who cut their way with swords, killing one outright and wounding many and people were half crushed. It lasted from 4 pm until 1 o'clock in the morning. The coffee houses where the largest crowds were to be found were attacked; windows were smashed on the Marienplatz. There was a mention of it in the papers but for the most part it was kept secret.

It did say that,'unfortunately the soldiers helped the women and children'. This is how women and children are being treated while their fathers and sons bleed for this rotten business. They are beginning to say that should the enemy come we would do better under the French, for it is not going well with the wretched rabble. We in the country are not yet complaining, but those in the towns do so.

A poster depicting a life-style that was fast disappearing in austerity wracked Germany. A poster for the Regina Palace Hotel, Munich.

Extract from a letter from an NCO, 257 Signaltrupp X Corps

I was pleased to hear you were safe and sound and hope you will soon be lucky enough to be sent to the Russian front as, except during a few critical days when the Russians gain ground by throwing endless numbers of troops against our front, one is better off here than on the France side. Sometimes they have so many men that they attack our positions without even artillery preparation. The only disagreeable point of the operations is that when the left and right have to give up their positions we also have to fall back.

Extracts from prisoners' letters taken in the Pozières sector

5 August 1916

Here there is no post only shells. It's misery. The minutes become hours, the hours days and a day here is an eternity. Things are going badly with us; the last meal we had was dinner yesterday and there is nothing at all here to drink. When we can get out of these trenches we have no idea. In front and behind us and on one side are the English. What will become of us I don't know if our people don't come to our aid from the rear so that we can withdraw. Otherwise

German prisoners being searched for that bit of written or printed information that will be worth translating and passing on to headquarters.

those who are left of us, and are spared, will have to go to England.

4 August 1916

Things are bad. Yesterday morning we entered the trenches and in the evening had to beat off an attack by the English. It is horrible. I was completely depressed, but who troubles about such a thing here? It is indeed hardly worth calling a trench, it is more of a sap. We have always to lie down or sit, we cannot stand for then we would be seen. You can't imagine how grateful I would be to God if peace came. I am desperately homesick, but I must stay here and take the consequences.

An order found on a German prisoner – behaviour in the front line so as to avoid drawing fire

17 August 1916

Everyone is to find himself a hole and is not so much to show his nose, except the sentries detailed. The enemy bombardment was exceptionally heavy this morning and was due the fact that officers and men of the 8th Company, II Battalion, 104th Regiment were swarming about and making themselves at home. This will not do, we are at war. Every movement is seen by enemy aircraft or from the nearby village of Longueval. For this reason the trench must appear deserted. The standing about of servants, orderlies and relieving sentries is forbidden. Strict non-movement is to be maintained. Every offender will be brought before the Military Tribunal and, if necessary, I shall take steps to obtain obedience by force.

Extract from the diary of a Prisoner of the 125 Regiment

22 August 1916

For the last two days we are again sitting in the line, this time in a fresh and worse sector. Since darkness fell they have been bombarding ceaselessly, tomorrow at dawn they may try to attack. However, they will not be successful. Our position consists mainly of shell holes in the sides of which small holes are dug. Someone frequently gets buried and then it is a case of digging them out. He can be thankful if he escapes with nothing more than a fright. Thirst torments us terribly. Rations can be obtained for four days, but this cannot be done with water, so it is simply a matter of enduring.

For the last few days I have been in temporary command of our company. In the two days that we have been in the line we have suffered thirty casualties. Thank God that only two of that number were killed.

In daylight one hardly dares to be seen in the trench due to the British aircraft. They fly so low that it is a wonder that they do not pluck someone clean out of the trench. Nothing is to be seen of our brave German flyers despite the excellent ratio of our sixty-one aircraft to their twenty-nine. One can hardly calculate how much additional loss of life and strain on the nerves that this costs us. I feel doubtful regarding the final outcome of our good cause when such poor fighters are there to champion it.

No one out here needs to be foolhardy, but everyone has the duty and responsibility of so carrying out his duty so as to be able to answer to his conscience.

Another two men buried and, fortunately, dug out again safely.

XV Corps

German prisoner's letter – Pozière Sector

One is no longer a man here, one is worse than a pig, filthy from top to toe, even worse than on the Lorette Ridge. For you the beastly war is at an end, so don't take it too much to heart concerning the loss of your left arm. The most important thing is to be far, far away from here, for one can scarcely look any longer at the misery and

Reinforcements and some returning from leave carry parcels to the front.

distress. If the people at home could just see this, perhaps there could be an alteration, but they are never told. Not until the tenth day did we get any food, which was, however, no longer warm but cold. Even the coffee we received was cold. When you get thirsty you must drink. However, the gentlemen, the officers seem to get something to eat and drink. The poor rank and file, apparently, they don't need it, after all they may get killed, one after the other, while the others [officers] sit in shell-proof shelters a safe distance from their companies.

Now it is the eleventh day that we have been sitting in this horrible filth and have been waiting day after day for that longed for relief, but as if the world had conspired against us, we still have not been relieved and always more losses. The company will shrink to one single bunch if we are not relieved soon. We each crouch in a little hole that we have dug out for ourselves as a protection from possible splinters and stare at nothing but the sky, and the back wall of the trench. Aircraft circle over us and try to do some damage. But only enemy planes, for a German pilot would never dare to come here – far too dangerous – they're safely behind the lines and never do they appear here. What a great crowd!

A detail of about forty men belonging to the 11th Company 127th Regiment were on one occasion nearly all wiped out whilst taking up food to the 8th Company in the front line.

Orders have now been issued by the Germans in this sector that rations for the whole period that men are in the trenches are to be taken up by them and no ration parties are to be sent back.

German morale
An aspirant officer of the 204th Division captured 13 August had been wounded at Becelaere in 1914 while serving with the 26th Reserve Jäger Battalion. He had been in Germany ever since and had volunteered for this new division the moment that he heard that it was being formed, hoping thereby to get a commission. In discussing the war he admitted frankly that no right minded German had any further hopes of victory. Fears of an ignominious peace are beginning to creep in. The last reserves are now been drawn upon. He said that the morale of the German people, especially the saxons, had completely collapsed and that it was only the Government's iron hand that kept things going. He himself was loth to admit all this, but a stage had been reached when the true state of affairs could no longer be kept a secret.

Letter from a man of the 125th Regiment, 26th Division

18 August 1916

We have lost thirty casualties already in just two days.

Letter from a man probably of the 125th Regiment, 26th Division

14 August 1916

We were relieved on the 12th (eight days and nine nights ago). Unfortunately we leave here again tonight despite our numerous sick men who have also to go with us. The whole division and in fact the whole corps, have diarrhoea (*durchfall*). We have lost so many comrades killed and wounded, and now we have to go in again. We have real English in front of us, and have orders to take no prisoners and to despatch them all with the bayonet. Not a bad idea, but they get prisoners from us too, and what will they now do with them?

Letter to Musketeer Storz 125th Regiment, 26th Division

10 August 1916

Flozlingenn, near Rottweil [Württemberg]

A German card depicting the town centre at Rottweil.

On the 8/9 August a hostile aeroplane flew over the Powder Factory at midnight. Five men are said to have been wounded. Some are dead. One man had his shirt blown clean off and survived.

Letter to Musketeer Heuth 125th Regiment, Feldpost 26

10 August 1916

Rottweil [Württemberg]

Yesterday at 12 o'clock a hostile aeroplane was here and dropped three bombs and there were three dead and many wounded. Father is on night shift this week and came home at 2 o'clock in the morning. That was the night in the town of Rottweil, one million's worth of damage being caused by the Powder Factory affair.

Extracts from the diary of an officer of the 127th Infantry Regiment, XIII Corps. Left the Ypres front 29th July for the Somme

British newspaper report of the bombing of Rottweil by the RFC.

1 August 1916

Tremendous confusion prevails generally at the front: we cannot get to our position. Leutnant Pfleghar who has been from the company to the Battalion HQ says that the Battalion commander knows nothing at why men are lying around all mixed up, Jäger, 22nd, 19th in holes and shell holes. Saxons are coming here too, with whom the field police are having a tough job, as they are having to bring them out of the corn fields. So it is no wonder if there is nobody at the front.

2 August 1916

The French aviators fly scarcely 400 feet above our lines while not a single one of ours shows himself. We cannot fire at them for if we do we immediately attract heavy artillery fire. So we have to put up with it – lying in a trench in boiling heat, not moving and waiting until we are shot to pieces, buried, or, if God wills it, come out of it safely.

6 August 1916

Our airmen are so inferior that they do not operate from a field close to the front. Our standard of airmanship is far below the French and the English. In consequence we cannot go a yard outside the protecting cover of the foliage of the wood. Enemy aircraft are nearly always cruising round our bit of the wood spotting and signalling. In this particular aspect, we have to admit, whether we like it or not, we are outclassed. 'Germany ahead in the air' is not the case at all. That is why we have these enormous losses at the

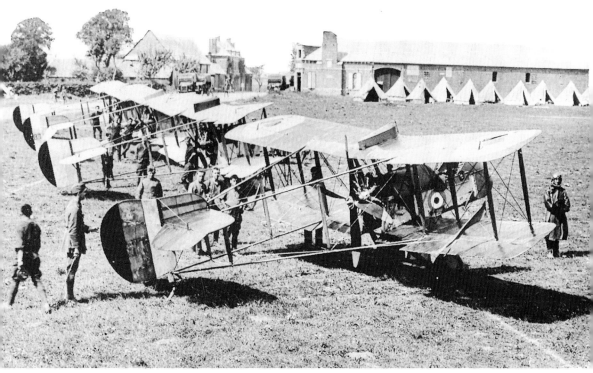

The airfield at Vert Galand in the summer of 1916 and a line up of DH2s of 32 Squadron. British and French squadrons effectively harassed the German troops manning the trenches.

front. No-one shakes off the pests which stick to us continually all day and into the evening. This moral defeat has a bad effect on us all.

8 August 1916

In order to keep the company together, should the bombardment of the wood be repeated, every squad, to-day constructed a trench which it is occupying. Numbers of deserters are multiplying frighteningly; yesterday one man of the company bolted as far as Equancourt where the Town Commandant arrested him and then telephoned the battalion. These fellows are making the regiment a laughing stock. Another soldier definitely stated that he would not go into the trenches anymore. All Hauptmann Göz's powers of persuasion proved unsuccessful. The number of men reporting sick is also mounting up. Leutnant of Reserve Schenk reported himself sick – foot trodden on. Some of our men are absolute cowards, who take every opportunity to get away from the company.

10 August 1916

Combles

The 2nd and 3rd Companies relieved the 5th and 6th in Combles

German underground artillery headquarters based in the château cellars and catacombs at Combles.

shortly after midnight. The men are in the trenches which lead through the houses and cellars. The officers and all the higher staffs are in the catacombs, which were only discovered when the civilian population took refuge in them when Combles was bombarded.

They are about fifteen metres (45 feet) underground. Combles presents a scene of the most fearful destruction and barbaric fury. We are partly to blame, as we have many gun emplacements in among the houses in the eastern part of Combles. However, the north-west part has also suffered severely.

Translation from a German document

Found last night (24th)

III Battalion HQ (76th Infantry Regiment) Battle HQ

24 August 1916

Heavy artillery fire of all calibres light, medium and heavy during the afternoon. The attack as far as observed was not extensive and collapsed in our splendid counter-barrage. As regards the total casualties there are no lists available. The 9th Company lost six killed and twenty wounded. Please send transport to the quarry for seven severely wounded. Every endeavour must be made to have drinks sent forward.

The 9th Company urgently requires bombs [hand-grenades].

The morale is good; the calls made upon the men are extraordinary.

Hostile aircraft are observed at a height of 100 to 200 metres and directing machine-gun fire at us and signalling with a horn.

Signed Hubner

Extracts from the Diary of Leutnant Karl Bopp
2nd Company, 127th Infantry Regiment.

1 August 1916

Things are in a terrible muddle and until order and central control are re-established there can be no question of a methodical counter-offensive. Our aviators are a poor crowd – not a one ever comes over our lines. The heat is most oppressive and most depressing. What must it be like in the front lines – in a shell hole with no shade? French airmen circle 200 metres above our lines while not a single one of ours puts in an appearance. We dare not fire at them for fear of being shelled in return. We must content ourselves with remaining in our trench – which is like an oven – dying of thirst and expecting to be either killed or buried by shells.

For food we have tinned meat, but there is no water – the nearest is in Combles which is under fire.

3 August 1916

Yesterday some went to Combles to get coffee, but it was no easy job

A shell-battered street in Combles, 1916. The original caption reads: Combles während der Beschiessung (*Combles during the bombardment*).

to get it back here. The soil here is composed of clay and chalk, it is excellent ground for digging dug-outs in, but in a 'cave' chances of getting out alive are poor. Yesterday I was very pleased to be able to dig out a man who had been buried.

The French are only firing big stuff (12 inch - 30 cm) pounding us all day long, artillery spotting being carried out most effectively by their airmen, while ours are nowhere to be seen, while the French are masters of the air.

4 August 1916

Hostile artillery bombardment all day. The air vibrates to shell bursts incessantly. All the firing is directed by the French aviators. They are fine fellows flying about 400 metres above our positions, but we dare not show ourselves or heavy artillery fire is immediately brought to bear on our trenches. If only our airmen were here the state of affairs would be different, and the enemy would not be able to lay down fire so accurately.

What purpose have the French in view, throwing away such quantities of ammunition? Their offensive has been checked they cannot advance further.

5 August 1916

A terrible day as at 11 am the French began a bombardment with guns of all calibres.

A letter from Ivan Pestorious, wife of a government official told him that my 'Chief' an old friend, Wiener, had been killed 27 July. In my muddy burrow I cried as I would have done had I lost my brother – a deep feeling of sorrow and hatred against the English, the criminal hand of whom had caused his death, fills my heart.

6 August 1916

The battalion was relieved under fairly difficult conditions. Unfortunately several more were wounded. Our airmen are so inferior, that even right behind our lines they do not have supremacy in the air. Their courage and daring cannot be compared to the English and French, in consequence we dare not set foot outside the foliage above us that hides us. Enemy planes are always cruising round the wood where we are and would report our position. Say what you will it is evident that we are their inferiors in this aspect. There is no one to drive away the parasites which dog us from morning to night. It certainly demoralises everyone.

The situation is more astounding when one takes into consideration the number of French planes we supposedly are bringing down, when they are always there above us in the same numbers.

A Field altar prepared for a religious service at Flers, on the Somme.

9 August 1916

10.45 Church Service

It was not by mere chance that the chaplain dwelt on faith and courage, and spoke of fear and cowardice. 'We owe a duty to our

Geh' o Soldat! und deine Pflicht erfülle!
Christus, der gute Hirt — bewachet seine Herden —
O Herr! Zukomme uns Dein Reich und gescheh' Dein Wille
Wie in dem Himmel, also auch auf Erden.

A. Setkowicz.

Popular postcard reassuring German troops that God is on the side of the Kaiser's armies and Jesus speaks German. The translation reads:

Go o soldier! and do your duty!
Christ the Good Shepherd keeps watch over his flocks.
O Lord! Let Thy kingdom come and thy will be done, as in heaven so on earth.

The familiar prayer men on opposing sides recited daily as they sought to kill each other and survive the carnage themselves. The belligerent men of God in their military uniforms had their work cut out convincing their respective flocks of divine favour and continuing support.

German Roman Catholic padre.

German Protestant chaplain.

84

„Ich will euch erquicken"

'I will refresh you' *reads the caption to this German postcard.*

conscience; to those who have shed their blood and fallen; to our folks at home. We hope we shall not have to remain longer than another week on the Somme, however, we shall only attain the end by perseverance.'

10 August 1916

Enemy airmen flying only 100 metres above us took part in the fighting using their machine guns. Men wounded in the head from above have been brought in. Leutnant Rickesen was taken prisoner by the English.

2nd Bavarian Reserve Infantry Division

Seven prisoners of the II Battalion, broke down the barricade about S2d. 95 in the intermediate line north-east of Bazentin-le-Petit, during the afternoon of the 25th and surrendered. They stated that they could no longer face our artillery fire which they described as 'unadulterated Hell'. They further stated that the affect of our trench mortar bombs was absolutely terrifying and very destructive to the trenches and personnel.

A letter written by a man belonging to the 2nd Infantry Ammunition Column, IV Army Corps

The IV Corps was at Bapaume from the beginning of July. We moved off on 11 July and while our Corps was in position we used to bring artillery ammunition but always at night. On the 24th our Corps was withdrawn from Bapaume again so much have they suffered.

Letter written from Cologne (VIII Corps district)

3 August 1916

At least 71,000 have been taken from Cologne in the last few days and all sent to the Western Front. Today we have got another 300 recruits of the 1917 Class, but all are strong fellows.

10 August 1916

Mannheim

Soon we shall have nothing more to eat; 300 gr of meat in the week – what is that? One egg, no more butter and little milk.

NCO's diary II Battalion, 121st Regiment

8 August 1916

At 5 am left 119 Regiment for Le Transloy. The whole way, twelve kilometres, under artillery fire. On the way we had to put on gas masks. We got for a time in trenches on account of artillery fire. At 10 am we fortunately got back, On the way we saw an artillery team which had received a direct hit – two men and four horses dead.

Is this a serious attempt to protect this mule against poisonous gas using a man's gas mask?

Poster advertising an exhibition in the city of Cologne (Köln) in aid of the wounded and disabled. Another example of how the war was affecting the nations, along with food shortages was the growing shortage of men; the captured letter tells of the 'Class for 1917 – next year's fighting manpower – being called up to serve in 1916. The poster reads:

Exhibition of war relief
War wounded: care, vocational training and education

9 August 1916

Rocquigny

Here on the Somme front it is awful. Day and night there is tremendous air activity and bomb throwing. Yesterday, 8 August, our Regimental Commander, Leutnant Oberst Keller, was killed.

12 August 1916

10 am march off to trenches to relieve. We have to make very great detours because every supply road is under heavy artillery fire day and night.

A man belonging to the I Battalion, 125th Regiment writes:

The 1st Company is rather weak as many men have diarrhoea.

Interrogation of a prisoner belonging to 7th Company, II Battalion, 118th Regiment, 56th Division

During our attack the four company officers escaped to the rear. The morale does not appear to be good as he states that the men in the trenches said that if the English came they would throw their rifles to the Devil and surrender, which a good many of them appear to have done.

Captured German document Field Artillery Regiment 13, 7th Infantry Division, III Mun. Column, XIII Army Corps

17 August 1916

We have our base camp in the château park in Mannancourt. Here in this breezy corner, things are very lively. It was much nicer in Werewick. I hope we shall not be here much longer as no troops could stand it for long.

Relatives and friends attend the funeral of a soldier who has died in the military field hospital at Mannancourt château.

Sheltering deep underground from the constant British barrage.

Extract from the *Vassische Zeitung*

Day and night in sunshine and in rain the English guns hurl their murderous lead across. Shells burst all around many of them exploding in front of our positions, where masses of enemy dead are lying. They fling up the torn-off limbs so that when the men have a chance to eat the very sight of meat is sickening to them. The noise tears to pieces all their nerves and senses; it drums incessantly on their ears so that a good many find their hearing completely gone. Worst of all are the enemy's heavy mortars. It is true they can be seen coming and one can get out of their way, but, as a guardsman told me, 'if a man runs away to the right there is an enemy airman above the trenches who tells their guns to fire more to the right, so the man has to run back to the left'. So it goes on; one is hunted up and down like a wild beast. There are times when our men curse and are homesick; but when the time comes for fighting, all these feelings disappear. Orders are given. A sense of duty and military discipline hold the men together; they are ready with iron resolve and bitter courage.

Found on a dead German belonging to the 179th Regiment, 24th Saxon Division

7 August 1916

Back in Beugny

Dear ones at home,

In this letter I can write and inform you where we are and what is before us. When you get this letter your son will either be dead or lying badly wounded and unable to send you word.

11 August 1916

Our I and II Battalions are already in the front line; we are in reserve for the time being, but we can't remain here too long on account of hostile aircraft and there would soon be trouble in the village. Now just a word about our own aeroplanes: really one must be almost too ashamed to write about them, it is simply scandalous. They fly up to this village but no further, whereas the English are always flying over our lines, directing artillery fire, consequently getting all their shells, including those of heavy calibre, right into our trenches. Our artillery can only shoot by the map as they have no observation. I sometimes wonder if they have any idea where the enemy's positions are, or even ever hit them at all. It was just the same at Lille, there they were, sitting in the theatre covered with medals – yet never to be seen in the air.

We are going up to the line to-night as far as I know, on the left of the Albert-Bapaume road. Our division's right flank is close to Pozières, our left High Wood. My regiment is on the left, but I don't know quite where.

In case of their death some German soldiers appear to have left a final letter to their families.

Captured letter

6 August 1916

Offenbach

How is the war going on where you are? Every day transport leaves here for Russia and trains are continuously going from France to Russia. What is going to happen there again? Already Offenbach has 5,000 widows and besides that there are also unmarried men who have fallen.

Letter from a man in the Naval Corps written from the Yser Front

7 August 1916

A few days ago a battalion of the 1917 Class arrived. They had received four months' training and have now come to our sector with their division. The are all young soft- looking fellows.

[3rd Guard Division suffered heavily in the Somme battle and at this point contains a large proportion of the 1917 call-up class.]

Youngsters (along with a couple of older NCOs) of Regiment 13, resplendent in their new equipment and rifles, parade for the front line. Calling up of the 1917 Class was viewed by the British as a significant sign of the drain the war was having on German manpower.

Extract from a letter from Hohensalza (II Corps district)

6 August 1916

Here the eighteen year olds are now being called to the colours.

Official German orders show:

1. In Lourach (XIV Corps district) boys of seventeen years of age were to be mustered as follows:

Born between 1.4.99 and 30.6.99 to report at end of August 1916

Born between 1.7.99 and 30.9.99 to report at beginning of October 1916

Born between 1.10.99 and 1.12.99 to report at beginning of January 1917

2. At Bamberg (II Corps district) lads liable for service in the Landsturm who were born before August 1899 had to appear on 1 September 1916 for enrolment

Mustering of the 1919 Class is going on throughout Germany.

Austrian Morale

Eight Czech regiments have been officially classified as 'Strafregimenter' ie punished collectively for breaches of discipline in the presence of the enemy. One of these regiments, the 28th, deserted with all its officers to the Russians in the Carpathians last year and has been struck off the rolls.

In addition to the above, another Czech regiment has been disbanded.

German Press

Karl Wegener writing in the *Kölnische Zeitung*

What now is to be seen is only that which has been possible to create under a fearful bombardment from both sides. These shell holes have become joined crater to crater. Men crouch in them for cover not daring to move at the mercy of the sun and the rain and not the slightest protection against the shells that drop from above. The men lie in these holes in the most fearful state of confusion; wounded who cannot be taken away until darkness falls and the dead who cannot be buried.

In the August heat the bodies of the dead begin to decay. The enemy incessantly strews the ground with shrapnel and rips it up with heavy shells. The enemy's airmen fly low over our positions and when they spot our men in the shell holes they signal back to observation posts in the rear to direct their gunners' fire with deadly accuracy upon our men. Or they themselves fire down on the men crowded in the holes. To convey warm food to the men lying out in the midst of these horrors is very seldom possible. Men crawl forward with food for their comrades each with a number of dixies fastened round their waists. Seltzer water has to be brought out to them also, for the scarcity of water to drink is proving one of the greatest trials. It even leads men to drink the dirty water in the shell holes, without considering what it may contain.

When an enemy attack begins the terror of these places go beyond description. Like the fiery rain of Gomorrah the artillery fire of the enemy comes down from heaven. The slight shelter afforded by the trenches and dug-outs is soon flattened out. With thundering roars the heavy shells from the enemy's gigantic mortars burst like volcanos, wiping out everything that was alive near the place where they explode. At the same time there falls a rain of shrapnel and poisonous clouds from gas shells roll forward.

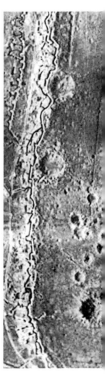

It seems there was no policy of playing down the horrors of trench warfare in the newspapers for the German public. Clearly defined German trench indicate the positions of the combatants with over twenty mine crate scattered through No Man's Land at this hotly contested part of the front.

Letters to the front

1 August 1916

Rodenkirchen, A/Rhein

> To-day a lot more have been called up – all the nineteen year old boys and very many old men.

13 August 1916

Plaeon

> Fritz is here on leave. He says that they [recruits] have to go to the front after only seven weeks training. Is this possible? The Hauptmann says that they are the last reserves.

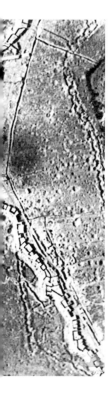

Extracts from statements of a prisoner of the I Battalion, 29th Infantry Regiment

On 12 August the prisoner had a conversation with soldiers of the 180th Infantry Regiment, when he went to Thiepval to fetch water for his wounded. He was told that the 180th Regiment was to be relieved and the prisoner replied that his Division expected the same. This gave rise to a discussion which ultimately developed into a quarrel. The soldiers of the 180th Infantry Regiment who are Württembergers said 'You damned Prussian swine have only just come into the line and are expecting a relief already, whilst we have been in this sector for months.'

The prisoner then replied: 'You damned Württembergers don't know what fighting is as you have so few casualties, whereas our Regiment is being wiped out.'

Extract from a letter

Bremen

It relates that when the *Deutschland* returned from America a part of the enormous crowd which had collected got onto to a landing stage, which collapsed under their weight. Many were thrown into the water and drowned and many others had their limbs broken.

Extract from a diary written by a man of the 73rd Fusileer Regiment, 111th Division

> The church has been turned into a hospital. It is always full of severely wounded soldiers. The mairie opposite the church is now an operating theatre. The churchyard is full of new graves – the

great offensive. Curiously enough there are very many artillery men buried here. The infantry are probably buried near the firing line. The artillery have suffered heavy losses. The airmen come down to as low as fifty metres and open fire on the gun crews. Once a battery has been located it can result in attracting 2,000 to 3,000 shells from enemy batteries. In this way we often lose guns.

The village of Ginchy has been utterly destroyed by artillery fire and there are no land marks left standing. There are no substantial trenches, only shell holes connected by shallow ditches.

Captured correspondence

20 August 1916
Hamburg

On Friday and Saturday there was an awful riot in the town. Several business men had their windows smashed in and their goods stolen. Here we are in the middle of summer and no potatoes are to be had. Vegetables and fruit are so expensive and can hardly be obtained. If only this misery was at an end. I cannot imagine what the winter will be like.

The police have been reinforced all over town and children are not

Busy port of Hamburg, despite the British blockade. Military inspectors checking the meat processing 'production line,' in the slaughterhouse of the cooperative at Hamburg-Hamm 1916. Tons of food for the fighting soldiers and precious little for the civilians.

allowed on the streets after 8 o'clock, and boys of seventeen not after ten. They may not gather and talk in the streets. In a number of streets everything has been smashed, cobblers, tobacconists, bakers – all smashed in. The bakers are so frightened that they selling bread without bread tickets. Now a special order has been declared giving everyone 250 grams of bread. Cart loads of potatoes (sixty-five in number) have been brought in. Where can they have been hidden? In any case we would only have got them when they were rotted. We were escorted to the door by soldiers with fixed bayonets. The 15th Regiment is quartered in the town.

Soldier writing from barracks

20 August 1916
Hamburg
Life here, as far as it goes, is pleasant, but we are always hungry, hungry, hungry. To-day, for the second time we are confined to barracks. We are 'Standing-to', which is absurd.

Extract from a letter

20 August 1916
Markneukirchen
This week the eighteen year olds who were sent home were again mustered. With the exception of cripples all were passed.

Some captured prisoners

During the last three days these prisoners received only one loaf of bread and a tin of meat and said that it was impossible to receive rations.

Deserter of the 5th Company, 35th Regiment, 56th Division

Prisoner stated that many more would come over if they were not informed that the English killed all their prisoners and that black troops were being employed by us.

Prisoner of the 5th Company, II Battalion, 88th Regiment

He lived for eighteen years in Switzerland and says that if he had any conception of what this war meant he would certainly have become a naturalised Swiss subject. He was extremely glad to have escaped from what he described as the 'massacre of human beings'.

The II Battalion of the Regiment received instructions to make a counter-attack and refused to leave their trenches.

Examination of two prisoners of the 5th Company, 35th Regiment, 56th Division

The II Battalion had been only three days in the front line. One of them stated that in their company, out of eighty-three who survived, only forty-three arrived in the front line. The rest had either been killed, wounded or deserted en route.

The morale appears to be very low. Half the men of the 35th and 88th have refused to go back into the front line. Prisoners told the story of an NCO who had refused to go forward. He was reduced to the ranks and sentenced to three years imprisonment. Hauptmann Hedemann, the battalion commander, had told them of this on parade.

Riots in Hamburg

20 August 1916

Yesterday it was war here also. Soldiers with bayonets were behind us. 15th Regiment is billeted in Hamburg. All the bread shops and butter shops, as well as some greengrocers' and grocers' shops were wrecked. Mother has just come and told us that mounted soldiers were met on the Mühlenweg.

Some of the troops stationed in Hamburg who had to quell the rioting citizens.

27 August 1916
Hennstedt

In Hamburg lately there has been a frightful commotion. The shops of Fietz and Herlbutt have been broken into and everything plundered, and bread stolen from the bakers. The greengrocers had to sell all their potatoes without tickets. It gets worse from day to day, principally in the 'Gross Staat'. Also at Tinn a hundred women marched through the streets. They all wanted to have more to eat.

For a fortnight we have seen no more butter. The times are continually getting worse. I do not know what will be the end of it.

19 August 1916

Here in Hamburg there has been a fearful riot to-night. Women and children have in Barenbach, Hofweg, Monckebergsten and other places broken into all the shops and partially robbed them. What is going to be the outcome? The people have nothing eat – no potatoes. Fat and bread are scarce.

Extract of a letter, man of the 86th Reserve Regiment, 18th Reserve Division

17 August 1916

We have been out of the mud for four days now and are resting at Vendegies-au-Bois [six miles north-east of Le Cateau]. Our Company has lost all its officers and 150 men, but that is usual for every company and regiment serving on the Somme. I, unfortunately, could not get the desired wound to have me sent home.

A person who lives in Holland near the frontier with Germany writes that every day deserters of all ranks, including officers, cross the frontier into Holland. These are not all recruits; many of them are hardened soldiers who have fought since 1914.

Extract from a letter written to a man in the 18th Bavarian Infantry Regiment

22 August 1916
Altenburg [Saxony]

Just think of it, your H went to a peace meeting yesterday evening. They are being held all over Germany. An enormous crowd turned up at the house where the meeting was being held and not everyone could get in. Well we were told how our government has made a mess of things and now they have no idea how to stop. How the diplomats have made a hash of things and the people have to suffer the consequences. But now we have had enough and grow weary of continuing shortages, while being expected to say nothing. A petition has been drawn up signed by the whole population and will be presented to the Prime Minister. It is difficult work but let us hope for success and if we do get peace, it will be due solely to the Social Democrats.

Feldmarschall **Paul von Hindenburg***

Born at Posen, 2 October 1847, son of Major Robert von Hindenburg. Entered *Kadettenhaus* at Wahlstatt in 1895 and the *Hauptkadettenanstalt* in Berlin in 1863. Joined 3rd Foot Guards Regiment at the beginning of 1866 as *Leutnant*. The 3rd Foot Guards had only just been formed at Danzig as sister regiment to the 1st Foot Guards Regiment.

At Koniggratz he distinguished himself by gallantly leading his platoon against a battery of guns which were captured, but had to be left on the field. For his gallantry *Leutnant* von Hindenburg received the Order of the Red Eagle, Fourth Class, with swords.

He took part in the Franco-Prussian war of 1870, and came unscathed through the battle of St Privat, in which the Guard Corps lost nearly three-quarters of its officers and he received a field promotion to adjutant of his regiment. He was present at Sedan and the siege of Paris.

He studied at the *Kriegsakademie* for three years and in 1878 became *Hauptmann* on the German General Staff; then G.S.O.2 of the II

Feldmarschall Paul von Hindenburg. Chief of the Imperial General Staff.

Army Corps (Stettin) and in 1881 G.S.O. of 1st Division (Königsberg). Here he studied frontier defenses, the narrow marshes and their passages. In 1884-85 he was attached for a year to a battalion of the 58th Infantry Regiment at Frandstadt (Posen) for frontier duty.

In 1885 he became lecturer on tactics at the *Kriegsakademie* in Berlin and was then G.S.O.1 of III Army Corps (Berlin) and then head of a

*Information on the enemy commanders was also included in the intelligence files of British Fourth Army.

department in the *Kriegsministerium*. In 1893 he was promoted to *Leutnantoberst* and was given command of the 91st Infantry Regiment at Oldenburg. In 1896 he became C.G.S. of the VIII Army Corps at Koblenz. In July 1900 he took command of the 28th Division at Karlsruhe. He commanded the IV Army Corps at Magdeburg from 1904 to the Spring of 1911 when he retired.

On 22 August 1914 he was appointed to the command of an army on the Eastern Front and days later leapt into fame by his victory over the Russians at Tannenberg. The reputation this success won for him in Germany was increased by the winter battle in the region of the Masurian Lakes, which terminated the second Russian invasion of East Prussia. During the offensive against Russia in the Summer of 1915 he led the Northern Group of armies and retained this command until the defeats suffered by the Austrians in June and July 1916 led to the command of all the German and Austrian armies in the east being placed in his hands. He had no opportunity however, of achieving anything in his new role, as at the end of August he was appointed Chief of the Imperial General Staff in succession to General von Falkenhayn.

Extracting information from prisoners – the German way; detailed instructions may be examined in this captured document. British prisoners, some wounded, await interrogation.

Extract from a captured document

HQ Group Kirchbach I.C.H. 34185

28 August 1916

Upon capture all prisoners must be taken from the divisions at once and marched to the prisoners' cage at Heuville. The escort must

British wounded prisoners in a dressing station – a study in disconsolation. These men would present possibilities for gleaning information during any interrogation by their German captors.

take all precautions to prevent the prisoners from destroying letters, orders etc, for they may prove to be of the greatest importance.

All papers taken from prisoners are to be handed over at Group Kirchbach. Money, watches, pay books etc are to be retained by the prisoners. Indications of rank, unit and articles of equipment, which are often taken as souvenirs, are to be left with them. When these items are removed identifying the unit to which the prisoner belongs often becomes impossible. This order applies also to wounded prisoners in dressing stations.

For the Army Group chief of the General Staff
von Franzenburg

Austria–Hungary

In order to reduce the consumption of meat the internal parts of the animals, such as tongue, heart, liver, kidneys, lungs, stomach etc will be considered to be meat in the proportion of one kilogram of the latter to one half kilogram of meat.

An order from the Austrian General HQ prescribes that in view of the scarcity of leather, all troops which have no marching to do will be equipped with wooden instead of leather boot soles.

Letter from Hamburg
20 August 1916

Here in Hamburg conditions are very bad at present. There are demonstrations here in the evening, principally in Barmbek. All the shops stocking fats have been wrecked there, and the 96th Regiment is always on stand-by ready to turn out. This was bound to happen for we shall soon not be able to afford the high prices. While the rich people indulge themselves as before. That also is quite wrong – meat is only for us to look at.

Today a young man from the Socialists called with a petition to collect my signature. They have as part of their policy the terminating of this war. I have also signed and they purpose to present it to the Chancellor. If only it proves to be effective, for it has gone on far too long. But, unfortunately, I fear that they will not care one jot if the poor man is ruined.

If you want to buy anything, linen etc, you have to obtain permission from the police, then you always get something new – but never anything of quality.

Translation of a German document

22 August 1916

XXIII Reserve Corps, General Head Quarters I.a. no.3156
With reference to Army Order of 20 August 1916. I. a.
9/20 (G.H.Q. I. a. 3156)
1. Epaulettes are not to be removed.
2. In the event of future troop movements it may be
necessary to have the numbers clearly visible again.
These must not be torn off the epaulettes, but rather
covered over with sewn-on grey cloth. In cases where
the troops have no cloth available, that is, out of stock,
kept for repairs etc notice must be given to the
intendance officer of the Corps [Quartermaster].
3. In order to identify single units after the numbers
have been obliterated a coloured band or strip of cloth
2cm broad must be sown onto the epaulette near the
sleeve.

Numbers on picklehaube covers must be completely
obliterated. Where commanders' names are now shown
on vehicles they can be allowed to remain, but hereafter
vehicles will only show the initials of commanding
officers.
Signed von Kathen

By 1916 the German High Command was becoming aware of the need to minimise information available to the enemy. The number on the picklehaube cover and epaulette denoting regiment had to be obliterated. Officers' names were not to be painted on staff cars. This staff car is assigned to the commander of 26th Reserve Corps, Heavy Artillery.

Captured document
1st Reserve Guard Division

30 August 1916

Once more it must be pointed out that the positioning of anti-aircraft guns in the rear and near rest billets is absolutely necessary. In the case of enemy aircraft flying low, as it is reported that they often do, it must be feasible to bring them down. A belt of fire should be put up directly in front of them so that they have to fly through it. There is no possibility of success if the aircraft are aimed at directly.

Extract from an army order issued by the German High Command

29 August 1916

According to reports that have come in from HQ, hostile airmen have sustained quite trivial losses from the machine-gun fire of our troops. The belief that hostile aircraft are protected by armour against infantry fire is incorrect. Concentrated fire at enemy aircraft has every prospect of success and must be carried out. Entrances to dug-outs must be concealed in order to render it difficult for enemy observers to see them.
Signed von Below

Captured German Order

30 August 1916

I have occasion to draw attention to the following:
The demanding for artillery barrage and the nervous firing of rifles, because an unseen bomber throws a few hand grenades reveals a state of nervousness. It brings no results and, to the contrary, causes only problems. We waste an enormous quantity of ammunition and when we want we are without. Secondly, we damage ourselves instead of the enemy. It has been constantly stated that troops have thrown an enormous quantity of hand grenades because they heard an enemy grenade explode somewhere.

I want this sort of thing stopped. It does us a lot of damage. The men must remain calm and keep their presence of mind. I count on the help of my officers and sergeant-majors.

I have the impression that a few Englishmen throwing grenades from their trenches can thoroughly frighten a crowd of Bavarians.

This must not carry on like this. Why always silently acknowledge the superiority of the enemy without reason?

The Artillery Commander has assured me that the state of things cannot continue. Both his ammunition and guns are done for.

Only company commanders can order rapid fire or volleys of hand grenades. There are plenty of alert company commanders with presence of mind. If troops open rapid fire on their own it only shows lack of discipline or despicable cowardice. If we put an unnecessary barrage on the enemy's trenches he retaliates, therefore, we suffer for it. Instead of demanding unnecessary barrage or wasting hand grenades it is much better if we do something useful, strengthen our wire entanglements, deepening our trenches and build strong shell-proof dug-outs for the garrison.

This fright on the Somme Front must be dispelled and calm must take its place.

Signed von Hassy Leutnant Oberst

Captured German letters

14 August 1916

Bayreuth

I heard yesterday that the Bavarians need 500 officers. We are bereft here as to-day 600 men are being posted to the 6th Bavarian Infantry Regiment (6th Bavarian Division), which is down to thirty-six officers and just fourteen men. Can this be true?

Two soldiers of the 19th Bavarian Infantry Regiment throwing grenades towards the enemy trenches, or in the view of Lieutenant Colonel von Hassy – wasting them.

Translation of a leaflet found on a German prisoner

To the inhabitants of Altenburg

20 August 1916

On Sunday, 20th August, and succeeding days the people of Altenburg will be visited at their homes by representatives of the Party and of the Trade Unions in order to give them the opportunity of signing a Peace Petition.

To ensure the speedy collection of signatures we herewith present the wording of the petition to the people of Altenburg and it reads as follows:

Petition

To His Excellency the Imperial Chancellor,

Dr von Bethmann Hollweg.

The undersigned demand that the speediest possible end be made of the war, which has devastated Europe for more than two years and which has imposed enormous sacrifices in blood and money upon the belligerent nations.

The undersigned reject all plans of conquest, which not only prolong the war, but also sow seeds for future conflicts. The undersigned require that the governments of the Central Powers make it known that they are ready to conclude a peace agreement which guarantees the Second Reich:

1. its political independence
2. its territorial integrity
3. freedom for its economical development.

The Committee of the Social Democratic Party

Extracts from captured letters

31 August 1916

Dear...

What do you think of Romania coming into the war. One could begin to begin to get discouraged as, at present, there seems to be no end in sight. For some days there has been a rumour that Russia intends to conclude a separate peace with us, but I doubt it. Perhaps they might have done had not Romania come in. You cannot begin to imagine the effect Romania's declaration of war has had on the public. Business has come to a standstill.

Dear Karl,

How much longer will the war last? There can be no thought of an end when one nation after another join in. One certainly thought

that Romania would remain neutral. How long before Greece becomes involved? Then there is still Norway and Sweden who will doubtless come in. There is no longer any talk of Germany winning. It might be the case that the war will cease all the sooner if they do come in. But there is no way of knowing for sure.

Romanian troops on the streets of Bucharest following the declaration of war on the side of the Allies.

Captured Battalion Orders

17 August 1916

A patrol sent out by the 5th Company comprising seven men (names follow) succeeded last night in wounding an English soldier in front of this Company's sector. Although they failed in their endeavour to bring him into our trenches, they were able to identify his regiment. The patrol acted with great determination.

As a reward, all members of the patrol are awarded ten Marks each out of canteen funds.

17 August 1916

The 5th and 7th Companies will take over without delay two boxes of S.A.A. containing 1,100 rounds each of 'K' cartridges (armour piercing). These are to be brought to the Battalion Command Post. Attention is drawn to the fact that 'K' cartridges may only be used with rifles with telescopic sights, and only at a range not exceeding 1,000 metres.

Chapter Four

The Month of September 1916

Extract from the British XV Corps Summary

2/3 September 1916

During the 1 September the enemy maintained their hold on the east corner of Delville Wood. Strong bombing attacks, accordingly were arranged to drive them out of this part. At 11.45 am our own bombers started advancing and pushed along the edge of the wood northward advancing to within fifty yards of Hop Alley, but it was found that there were a number of the enemy dressed in British uniforms and hiding in shell holes at the edge of the wood. These fired continuously on our advance and as it was impossible to distinguish the enemy from our own men, the attack was not able to progress any further. On three occasions officers went forward to take on their men and were, in each case, hit by the Germans whom they imagined to be their own men.

A German trench in Delville Wood.

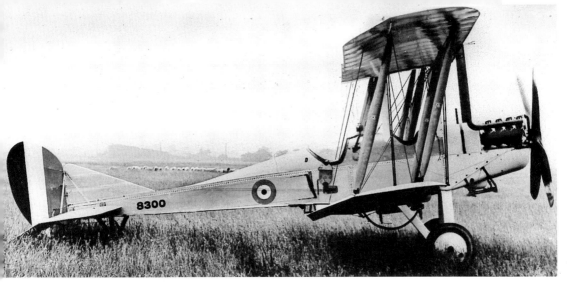

The BE2 C was the main aircraft employed by the Royal Flying Corps in the first three years of the war.

Extract from No.34 Squadron Royal Flying Corps records

3 September 1916

Bombs dropped on battery at N19 C99 to N19 D36. Four guns attacked by hostile aircraft over this battery. Descended to 2,200 feet and opened fire with machine gun on above mentioned battery. Battery ceased firing.

Captain Blount and Second Lieutenant Peason

Extract from Fourth Army summary

4 September 1916

Lieutenants Pollard and Scaife, seeing that own infantry were being held up by a German machine gun, attacked it from the air and this enabled our infantry to continue the advance. Falfemont Farm, south-east corner, big attacks by French and British on 3 September.

A message sent by 3 Company, 164th Regiment to I Battalion

3 September 1916

Please send up a reserve platoon as soon as possible to remove the large number of seriously wounded lying here. The Company is unable to cope with their evacuation.

Extract from the diary of a man of the 76th Regiment, 111th Division

III Battalion during the attack suffered many casualties; the 9th Company alone lost 120 men, though mostly wounded. III Battalion

about 500 men in three days. No trenches in the front line, men lie in shell holes, but the enemy aircraft descend to about 80 metres and strafe them with machine guns. They also signal their position to the artillery. Enemy aviators are far superior, especially in numbers. Our pilots are powerless and flee as soon as the enemy machines approach our trenches. Many air battles take place. About eighteen enemy captive balloons are up and about; two of ours are to be seen, as a consequence enemy artillery fire is tremendous. English aviators are often over our wood and we have to try and dodge them, we are always having to hide from them, yet they seem to find us out. Lively artillery fire in the evening, mostly 15 cm shells, we seek cover in dug-outs over six feet deep. No sooner do we retire to our quarters to try and get some sleep when they begin shelling us again and we have to don gas masks and seek cover in the dug-outs. We are all suffering because of it. Many are ill with diarrhoea.

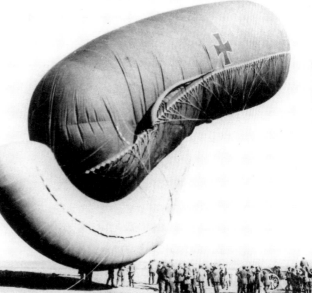

German Army observation balloon, with a crew of two, prepares to make an ascent. Note the parachute in case of an attack by British or French fighter planes.

Captured documents. No8a 10th Infantry Brigade

9 September 1916

To III/14th Bavarian Regiment and the two resting companies of 19th Bavarian Infantry Regiment in Le Mensil.

The III/14th and the two resting companies of 19th Infantry Regiment in Le Mensil will hold themselves ready to move off at a moment's notice. In case the roads to Le Transloy are unfamiliar they are to be reconnoitred.

Receipt of this order is to be acknowledged to 10th Infantry Brigade.

Austro-Hungary

A captured order of the Headquarters Staff on the South-West Front (11 March 1916) directs that polished steel shall universally be used in place of nickel in the manufacture of surgical instruments. Several army orders have been found recommending economy in the use of alcohol. The army ration of wine has lately been reduced from half to a quarter of a litre. An order of the Fifth Army (26 July 1916) forbids the use of light petrol in engines which can be run with heavy petrol.

British III Corps Heavy Machine Gun Section

Prisoners captured by the III Corps all agree that the Heavy Section MG Corps produced the most terrifying effect. In Martinpuich they moved about knocking down houses and destroying dug-outs. Prisoners said however, that they invariably shot too high.

A runner of the 133rd Reserve Regiment said that on the night 14/15th he carried a message from the regimental headquarters. This message warned the officers in the line to be on their guard against a British attack on the next morning, as armoured vehicles had been observed coming up the line. The observation was probably made from captive balloons or by aeroplanes.

15 September 1916
Bourlon

Headquarters of the First German Army (General von Below) were bombed to-day. Four bombs hit the château.

Prisoner interviews

Prisoners of the 2/7th Bavarians gave the following account of their attack at 6.30 pm on the 15th inst. The II Battalion attacked north of

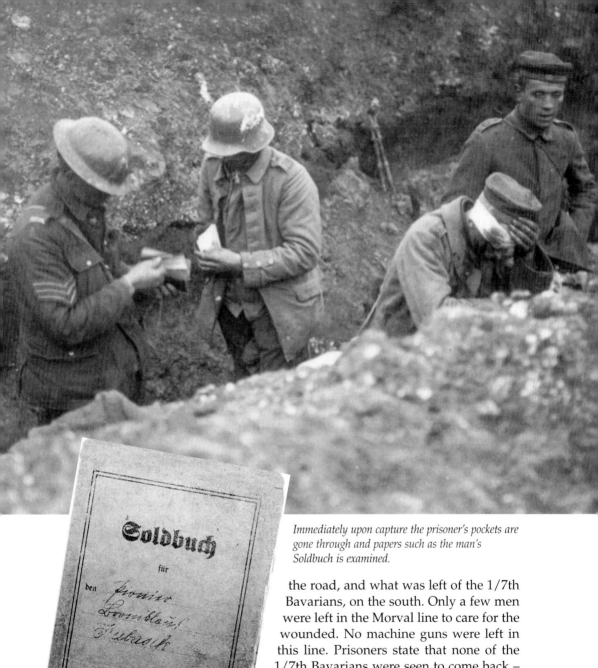

Immediately upon capture the prisoner's pockets are gone through and papers such as the man's Soldbuch is examined.

the road, and what was left of the 1/7th Bavarians, on the south. Only a few men were left in the Morval line to care for the wounded. No machine guns were left in this line. Prisoners state that none of the 1/7th Bavarians were seen to come back – all were either killed or taken prisoners. Very few of the II Battalion got back after their attack.

German Army Order

13 September 1916

The positions are to be held under all circumstances and at all costs. Large reinforcements are on their way. This order to be delivered to the front line immediately and where possible to be made known to all troops.

From a man of the 68th Reserve Infantry Regiment, 16th Reserve Division

15 September 1916

On the first day we lost over half of our Company. Our Battalion Staff were wiped out in the morning as they moved into position.

Maggot-ridden German dead still needed to be frisked for information.

From a man of the 10th Bavarian Regiment, 6th Bavarian Division

25 September 1916

We have had ten days hard fighting with the English. The 1st Company has again had many casualties. Corporals Schiller, Wagner, Taubmann, Geer, Stark and Neumeur dead, and many others wounded. It is simply dreadful what our Regiment has had to go through.

From a man of the 2nd Bavarian, 238th Reserve Infantry Regiment, 52nd Reserve Division

25 September 1916

This is no longer regular warfare, but more like murder. I ask you, what is there is left to fight with when a company 180 men strong, in the course of a few hours, melts away to between forty and fifty men?

From a man of the 229th Reserve Infantry Regiment, 50th Reserve Division

26 September 1916

Our Company [the 5th] had 107 casualties on the first day. It is still forty-eight strong with the new draft.

Diary of a man of the 9th Bavarian Infantry Regiment, 4th Bavarian Division

Describes the German gas attack east of Loos on 29 April 1916 in which the gas blew back over the German lines.

The III Battalion of the Regiment had about 500 gassed cases, a large number of whom died. On 1 May 1916 I went back with the 9th Company to rest billets at Esterelles. In my new billet three NCOs and four men were killed through a gas attack which miscarried. The 3rd Company lost fifty-six men.

German documents

The *Sturmtruppen* are specially trained for trench fighting, grenade throwing, getting over wire entanglements etc. They are therefore only to be used for special purposes with very clear planned objectives. Distributing detachments amongst the conventional infantry along the whole line in order to support the latter results in

Stormtroopers lined up for inspection prior to them going up to the front. Each man has a canvas bag filled with grenades. These specialist assault units would be increased in number and used to good effect in March 1918.

the dissipation of this force and is a misuse of its specialist training. *Sturmtruppen* support the attack, but on account of their limited numbers cannot, of course, carry it through alone. It is most advantageous to put them in position near the enemy where the possibility of a surrounding or flanking movement exists.

Every *Sturmtruppe* will be accompanied by one or two selected infantry sections with as many hand grenades as it is possible to carry. Together with these, the *Sturmtruppen* will form the first wave of an attack.

Once the attack is carried through the *Sturmtruppe* should be withdrawn as soon as possible, so as to spare them and maintain their fighting efficiency. They are not to be used for the purpose of defence.

Baden 238th Reserve Infantry Regiment
MG Company
Leutnant Schwanocke, *Sturmtruppe* Officer
For Army Chief Command, Chief of General Staff, Loesberg

Prisoners' comments

According to a prisoner of the 17th Bavarian Infantry Reserve Infantry Regiment when our men are taken prisoner they are stubborn and sulk and know little in any case. The German prisoners express surprise that our officers go on patrols.

RUMANIA'S DAY

THE TWO FORCES

KAISER: "So you, too, are against me! Remember, Hindenburg fights on my side"
KING OF ROUMANIA: "Yes, but freedom and justice fight on mine"

Reproduced by special permission of the Proprietors of "PUNCH"

British comment on Romania joining the Entente against the Central Powers in August 1916.

3 September 1916

Dear...
What are they saying about Romania where you are? The Greeks are sure to join too. Then only America and Switzerland will be missing.

5 September 1916

How have the swine drawn in Romania? Who knows who will be next? England ought to sink into the ocean by means of an earthquake.

7 September 1916
Nurnberg

Then there are the recent political disturbances. Romanians disgraceful conduct. What do these English diplomats not accomplish? They will not rest until they have set Europe's entire pack of hounds upon us.

15 September 1916

Fifteen German aircraft and two balloons were destroyed.

16 September 1916

Picklehaube bearing the inscription 'Waterloo' were recovered in a raid south-east of Bois Grenier on the night 15/16th September. This battle honour is worn by a few Hanoverian regiments, including the 77th and 78th Landwehr Regiments.

5th Battery, 5th Bavarian Field Artillery Regiment

Prisoners state that they had suffered severely from our artillery bombardment which they described as being more than human beings could stand for more than a few days.

For their Flying Corps they had the utmost contempt, and for our

A 77mm M96 field gun on a makeshift ramp takes on an anti-aircraft role and is manned by a crew of eight.

Royal Flying Corps they expressed great admiration. They have now started using field howitzers for shooting at our aeroplanes.

German pigeon message

14 September 1916

To 4th Bavarian Division 4.15 pm.
Enemy artillery is very heavy; our artillery firing back but little. Our aircraft not to be seen. Enemy attack anticipated.
III Battalion 9th Bavarian Infantry Regiment

The German newspaper *Neue Freie Presse*

Anyone would think that the objective of the British and French was to kill as many Germans as possible every week or every month. They have no tactical ideas, they are simply for butchering us.

116

Captured documents

24 August 1916

Among German documents captured by the XV Corps is one signed by the Chief of the General Staff of the Army in the Field, von Falkenhayn: No.33433, stating that the consumption of guns and ammunition is, through various causes, exceeding the supply and the reserves are being diminished.

Methods of overcoming this grave state of affairs are dealt with and in particular the following points are to be observed:
1. Retaliation and so called liveliness shooting must be reduced to a minimum on quiet fronts.
2. The time over which barrages extend must be reduced.
3. Light damage to guns must be repaired right away. Useful life of the piece is increased in this way.

Unposted letter of an officer of the 14th Bavarian Infantry Regiment

Since yesterday we have been continually bombarded by gas shells and scarcely get our masks away from our faces than we are forced to put them on again. Isn't that the limit?

We are alright so far, but we live and look like pigs and that is the least of our troubles. Here we have a so-called 'Bau Company' [Pioneer Company] which does most everything but build – that is absolutely impossible here.

Let us hope the worst is over, if not, still we won't lose heart for a long time yet.

There are no signs of Hauptmann von Hass, probably he is wounded or has been captured. Echerlein got killed. The battalion still has six officers left.

Pigeon message

14 September 1916

From III/9th Bavarian Infantry Regiment to 4th Bavarian Division 5.30 pm

Enemy artillery fire of all calibres on Section S.W. 9th Infantry Regiment increases from time to time to an intense bombardment. Flers and Wood B.B. position continuously under heavy fire of large calibre. 10th Company, 9th Regiment reports at 4 pm. Enemy trenches in front of Delville Wood thickly manned; our artillery is firing but spasmodically; no sign of our own aircraft.

Enemy attack expected.

The kite balloons ranged a battery on Les Boeufs church tower from which machine guns were firing. The tower was destroyed.

Captured German document

The following flare signals are applicable to the whole sphere of the German First Army:

    Request for barrage = Any red signal
    Lengthen range = Any green signal

German listening apparatus

According to the statement of prisoners the listening apparatus is run by the Corps and is manned by special personnel who are good linguists. They wear a letter 'T' on their epaulettes. These men are kept well behind the lines to reduce the probability of their capture. A prisoner also said that the use of telephones, except for urgent messages, is forbidden during alternate hours so as to facilitate the hearing of our messages.

Enemy ruses

On being interrogated a good many prisoners give as an excuse for not being able to answer our questions, that they have only recently returned to their regiments after a long spell in hospital. The men are probably instructed to answer in this way if they should be taken prisoners. Such a statement should always be verified by an examination of the prisoner's *Soldbuch*.

Captured message from II Battalion 212th Reserve Infantry Regiment

16 September 1916 12.30 pm

Casualties increasing on account of heavy artillery counter bombardment from the direction of Thiepval.

(It was probably sent from Feste Staufen or Feste Zollern.)

According to one source, German field telephones were not to be used during certain times so that a special detail, each man skilled in languages, could listening in to British and French telephone messages.

Message sent by Company Commander, 6th Company (211th Reserve Infantry Regiment)

11 September 1916

To II Battalion von Rege, (211th Reserve Infantry Regiment).

Company has sustained very heavy losses. and is no longer capable of holding this sector in the event of an attack. The losses are, in the main, to our own heavy artillery. Request that we may be relieved to-night. Leutnants Roettger and Slawinski and Feldwebel Hoffmann are missing. We have lost contact with troops on our right. We are still in touch with the 5th Company on the left. Leutnant Pazel has been seriously wounded. An attack on our position appears to be impending. Communication with our right is not possible since everything there has been flattened out.

Translation of a note written in the front line

13 September 1916

From 6th Company, 7th Infantry Regiment.
To II Battalion, 7th Infantry Regiment.
I beg to inform you, with some urgency, that our 15 cm howitzer battery is dropping shells on our position and nowhere else.
Anxiously awaiting the soda water.
Signed Schmidt

Message officer commanding 5th Company, II Battalion, 211th Reserve Infantry Regiment, to Battalion Commander

14 September 1916

I have assumed command in place of the seriously wounded Leutnant Pagel. I request, most urgently, that the Company be relieved. The spirit of the men is very depressed owing to the continual state of alert; the artillery fire and the terrible living conditions. As a consequence, the fighting value is very low.

A fully manned signal post. The instruction board for firing warning flares reads:
Light signals.
Red: Barrage
Green: Fire move forward.
White with ramification: Alert!

Extract from a letter
6 September 1916
Breslau

> Just think, from Breslau alone 16,000 men were drafted out to the front and reinforcements for these have already been called up.

Extract from a German diary
6 September 1916

Cambrai where the diarist comments on the activity and the trams. German walking wounded make their way to the railway station. Inset: trams in Camrai being used to transport wounded. These photographs were taken one month after the diarist visited the town by cycle.

> According to orders we moved off to Gouzeaucourt twenty-eight kilometres away. The wagon was loaded up at 7.30 am. At 9 am five of us went off on bicycles to Cambria. There we were halted at a German inn (*Wirtschaft*). Two glasses of wine and some dry bread bucked us up splendidly. The life and activity in Cambria was interesting to us, for it is a handsome and good-sized town and has various places of interest. There is an electric tramway system operating there. The market place 'Grande Place' is spacious and

every day vegetables, fruit etc are on sale. A pear costs the respectable sum of one mark. However, we could not find any sausage, cheese, or anything like that. Only cakes of microscopic size could be obtained at 40 pfennigs each. At about twelve mid-day we went on to Gouzeaucourt. The road is paved nearly all the way but so worn by traffic that speedy travelling on a bicycle is quite impossible. In fact cycling in this hilly country is very hard work. At 2 pm we arrived at Gouzeaucourt. Quarters had been arranged by the 11/14. We went into a house that was partially ruined and our quarters were on rotten boards. Already the well known trench smell was noticeable. The traffic here is tremendous. I operated the telephone exchange until 8 pm and then went for a walk. Weather is fine but misty.

7 September 1916

Moved on to Rocquigny where we arrived at 5 pm. Our progress was frequently held up by the enormous traffic of wagons, lorries, motor cars and formations of troops. The whole activity resembles that of Champagne in 1915. At 6 pm Rocquigny was shelled; thank God the shells either went over the village or dropped short and no lives were lost. In Rocquigny, with its sixty to seventy houses, there are are no less than two artillery and two infantry regiments. The thundering of the guns continue. The weather is fine.

Horse-drawn ammunition wagons and motorized transport throwing up dust through this Somme village.

The main street through Flers, September 1916.

8 September 1916

Aerial activity. Bombardment becomes heavier. Cacophony unceasing. Indescribable activity as troops come and go.

9 September 1916

The III/14th bivouacked here last night, whereas I/14th has already been three days in the line, and the II/14th one day. This morning at 3 am we set off for the front line. The route led over fields and meadows to Le Transloy. Our progress was very slow due to the numerous shell holes and the thick mist. In Le Transloy we bore to the left still following the route along the troop track. Unending ammunition columns passed us at a quick trot. Just behind Le

Transloy we received the first English greeting in the shape of heavy shells, the shooting becoming more and more lively and the air blackened by smoke. Noticeable was the smell of putrification which was so strong that we were obliged to march at the quickest pace in order to get out of that atmosphere as soon as possible. We went wrong several times until finally we reached Gueudecourt, a literal heap of ruins. from there we got to the main road to Flers, arriving there at 7.30. Immediately we looked around for a shell-proof cellar and succeeded in finding one. Flers is a total scrap heap and will probably be our quarters for the next sixteen days. It was not long before the mist lifted and the bombardment began on Flers. All calibres were fired into the place by both English and French. It continued in an unbroken thunder, absolute hell let loose.

10 September 1916

The III/14th moved last night into the sector of the 19th Regiment as storming battalion. The assault was to be directed from Ginchy in the direction of Delville Wood. Nothing further known so far. At 5.45 am I had to be ready to accompany the commander into position. From Flers a sunken road, heavily shelled, led us on to a large open space. Shelling is going on everywhere creating even more shell holes. Passing through numerous of our battery positions we at last reached the Gallwitz-Riegel [Gerd Trench]. It was here that we met General Jaeger, who was also to accompany us to the position. From the Gallwitz-Riegel to the Leiber-Graben which led us into the Second and First lines. The trenches were mostly revetted and men lay in niches which had been cut into the parapet. This primitive form of cover increases the likelihood of men being buried where they lie, hence the many missing. The stay in the heavily shelled position is very brief and, above all, dangerous. In the front line the men were only occupying shell holes. In addition there is the strong stench of putrification which is almost unbearable, that pervades the position.

Corpses lie, either inadequately covered with earth on the edge of the trench, or quite close under the bottom of the trench, so that the thin covering of earth allows the smell through. In some places bodies are in the open or trench recess for several days, quite uncovered and no one appears to be disturbed by this. Horrible sights are to be seen, here an arm, foot, or even a head sticking out of the earth – and these are all German soldiers – heroes, whom for the time-being no peaceful corner exists for them to lie undisturbed. Perhaps later when things are quieter they will receive a well-earned resting place, or perhaps not. Such is the soldier's lot.

Last night the III/14th under the command of Hauptmann von Haas made an assault in Delville Wood.

The diarist mentions the 'soldier's lot' and describes the awful conditions surrounding the ruined village of Flers in the late summer of 1916.

Nothing is yet known as to the result. So far 144 wounded of the III/14th have gone through Flers. Several officers are said to be dead or captured. According to statements by wounded it was a horrible affair.

12 September 1916

Got up at 1.30 am as I had been ordered back to Brigade at Le Transloy. We started out from Flers but it was impossible to get through the barrage. At last at 2.30 we succeeded in getting away. At 7.30 am we reached the Brigade safely. We remained at Brigade until 9 pm. We had to get back with orders to our Regiment at Flers through heavy fire. One could see wonderfully how the British use their *Flammenwerfer* and incendiary shells. Tomorrow we leave the battle HQ in Flers.

Feeling in Bavaria

A medical officer belonging to the 4th Bavarian Division stated that the present feeling between Bavarians and Prussians was far from good. The feeling was gaining ground that Bavarian troops were always sent where the heaviest fighting was going on. Bavarian losses had been far heavier in proportion to the population to those of other German nations. The prisoner stated that in his district (the Bavarian alps) 80% of the men at school with him had been killed or maimed for life. It was in order to counteract this feeling that the Bavarian Crown Prince and Prince Leopold of Bavaria had been placed in command of a group of armies on the Western and Eastern fronts.

The Prime Minister, von Bethmann Hollweg, had recently been to Munich to try and assuage the feeling of bitterness which was rapidly increasing. The morale of the men now being sent to the front was low, especially among the untrained Landstrum and Ergatz Reservists.

Russian Rifles

Several Russian rifles have been found in the old German gun position at R 36a. The German S.A.A. ammunition is not suitable for this rifle as the bolt cannot be closed when a round is in the chamber.

Prince Leopold Maximilian Joseph von Bayer of Bavaria.

Prime Minister, von Bethmann Hollweg.

Prisoners captured east of Courcelette

The morale of 393rd Regiment is very bad indeed – many men have absented themselves. One of the prisoners stated that they had given themselves up without firing a shot, because they could trust the English. The platoon commanders had gone away and the prisoner was to alert the platoon in case of an attack, but he did not do so on purpose. They fired neither rifles nor machine guns and they didn't throw bombs.

One of the prisoners was a 'Brother of Mercy' from a monastery and was exempt from active service. However, 24 July 1916, all the religious who had previously served were called up.

Prisoners (officers) including II Battalion, 6th Bavarian Infantry, Commanding Officer

The battalion had been in the line for more than six days and there was no likelihood of relief. They all agreed that our men attack with great dash and they were surrounded and cut off before they were able to realise that the attack had commenced. The effect of the artillery was awful and they almost welcomed the moment when the attack started, which meant that the bombardment lifted off their immediate vicinity.

They no longer expressed any belief in a German victory, but thought that England could not afford the sacrifice that such a battle as this entailed. They complained bitterly that their own artillery had left them in the lurch and could not understand the reason for it. Like every other German they expressed the greatest admiration for our RFC and complained about their own.

This morning at about 7.30 to 8 am a 'Tank' came creeping up behind them. The Battalion Commander decided then to surrender and ordered his men to lay down their arms, which seems to have pleased everybody. They were all delighted to be taken prisoner and glad to be out of the 'Hell of the Somme'.

According to the captured commander of the II Battalion he decided to surrender when a tank came creeping up from behind taking them by surprise. The noise of a tank on the move was reported to be deafening.

A direct hit on this German gun pit blew the weapon to pieces.

Prisoners II Battalion, 13th Bavarian Infantry Regiment

The morale of the 13th Bavarian appears to have suffered a good deal. They stated that all their officers had gone back from the front line with various excuses and the company was commanded by a sergeant major. (No officers of the 13th Bavarian were captured.)

The prisoner described the artillery fire as terrible; communications both forward and to the rear were nearly always cut. One gun pit of the 3rd Battery 11th J.A.R. received a direct hit, 24 September, blowing the gun right out.

Prisoners (officers) I Battalion, 6th Bavarian Infantry

26 September

They relieved men of the 10th Bavarian on the night of 19/20 September and expected to be relieved last night. They said that they were entirely out of touch with regimental HQ and up to the time they surrendered were carrying on the war on their own.

A man of the 2nd Company, I Battalion, 1st Bavarian Regiment, 5th Bavarian Division writes:

1 September 1916

Dear...

From the 12th to the 27th we were on the Somme and my regiment had 1,500 casualties; my company twelve to fifteen dead and wounded. At present we are digging for three days at Curlu where a third position is being constructed.

A man of the 9th Company, III Battalion, writes:

When I came to my present Regiment it had already been 'put in' on the Somme. They had 1,700 casualties.

A man of the 17th Bavarian Regiment, writes:

1 September 1916

We are actually fighting on the Somme with the English. You can no longer call it war; it is more murder. We are at focal point of the present battle in Jaureauor Wood. All my previous experience in this war, the slaughter at Ypres, and the battle in the gravel pit at Hulluch are the purest child's play compared with this massacre, and that is much too mild a description. I hardly think that they will bring us into the fight again now, for we are in a very bad way.

A man of the 3rd Battery, I Battalion, 16th Loiraine Foot Artillery Regiment writes:

2 September 1916

There are a great number of aircraft here. The water conditions are also extremely bad; most of the men are ill. These are the evils of war. I hope very soon we shall have the long desired peace.

Conversation with three officers 11th and 12th Companies, 11th Bavarian Regiment

The III Battalion, 11th Bavarian Regiment came into line about 1,000 metres west of Gueudecourt on the night of 26/27th. They relieved what was left of their other battalion. They described their losses as terrible, dead and mangled lying around everywhere, they themselves were in a dug-out. Anyone who attempted to leave was immediately killed or wounded. Before they realised that the New Zealanders were attacking they were in their trenches and they and the remainder of their company surrendered. They say they received the very best of treatment from the moment they were taken. They do not think that Germany can hold out over Christmas as their losses have been so enormous.

Diary of an NCO taken prisoner

27 September 1916

Woke at 8 am. Everything suspiciously quiet. Rations not half sufficient. Nothing to drink. Afternoon also quiet. Great hopes of being relieved and everyone very glad. Towards evening an English light signal fired close to us. Everyone feeling despair due to there being no support and no reserve. No light signals. All the men miserably weak. Had some water fetched. Slept well into the night due to sheer exhaustion.

Germans two to a bunk shelter from the constant Allied bombardment.

28 September 1916

No relief, feeling of hopelessness, apathetic, everyone sleeps under heaviest fire due to weariness. No rations – no drink. The whole day heavy fire on the left. We received heavy and high explosive shells. Everything is all the same to me. Best thing would be for the English to come. No one cares about us, our relief said to be cancelled. If one wants to sleep the aeroplanes will not allow one to rest. In the present conditions one no longer thinks. Iron rations, bread, biscuit, all eaten.

Translation of a portion of a XXVI Reserve Corps Order

I have to express my sense of recognition to the 10th Company 235th Reserve Infantry Regiment for destroying a hostile armoured vehicle [tank] and for removing six machine guns. This plucky and determined act was in keeping with the offensive spirit which has always characterised the XXVI Reserve Corps, against which all hostile attacks will break, both now and in the future. I look forward to receiving recommendations for the Iron Cross.

Surrender to aircraft

A contact patrol machine flew at 300 to 400 feet over Gird Trench in N 32. There Germans in the trench thereupon held up their hands and waved white handkerchiefs. The observer transmitted this information and the Germans shortly afterwards surrendered to our troops on the ground.

Translation of a German document

17 September 1916

A HQ. As regards the English and French attacks on the 4th and 12th instant, British prisoners make the following statements:
1. We were too slow in putting up a barrage. This was too far behind. The foremost attacking waves consequently were hardly touched by artillery fire.
2. Our troops were surprised in their dug-outs by the attackers.
3. The Second line was either only lightly manned and unoccupied. Weak counter-attackers were easily mastered and the undefended Second line crossed.
Signed von Lassberg, Oberst, Chief of General Staff

An extract from a captured German officer's diary found in Starfish Line, west of Flers, probably belonging to the 52nd Reserve Division

22 September 1916

The four days ending 4 September spent in the trenches were characterised by continual enemy artillery bombardment, that did not abate for a single instant. The enemy had registered on our trenches with light as well as medium and heavy batteries, notwithstanding the fact that he had no direct observation from his trenches which are on the other side of the summit. His registering was done by means of his excellent air service, which renders perfect reports of everything observed. During the first day, for instance, whenever the slightest movement was visible in our trenches, during the presence of enemy aircraft flying at 300 to 400 metres, a heavy bombardment of that particular section took place.

The very heavy losses during the first day were brought about by

Dominating the battlefield as a defensive weapon the MG08, with a firing rate of up to 40 rounds per minute and range of over 2,000 metres, was a formidable killing machine.

An infantry squad practice anti-aircraft drill for the benefit of the cameraman.

the order to evacuate the trenches during daylight. Only a small garrison was left, the remainder withdrawing to a part of the line on the left of the Martinpuich - Pozières road, which was hardly fired at. Here they took shelter in dug-outs disguised by branches of trees. It was possible to hold the trench in the day time with a small garrison, because the enemy's trenches were at a great distance, and the position was guarded by a machine gun on the flank. At nightfall the rest of the garrison returned and repaired the damaged positions as well as was possible under the artillery fire. By retiring from our trenches we reduced our casualties over the following days.

The signal for a bombardment by heavies was given by aeroplanes turning sharply towards their own lines and blowing a klaxon horn. On the first day we tried to fire by platoons at the aeroplanes, but a second aircraft retaliated by dropping bombs and firing his machine gun at our troops. Also increased shrapnel shells were fired at our positions. Our own airmen appeared only once for

Human remains were strewn everywhere on the Somme battlefields as the living awaited an opportunity to dig them into the ground. Then bursting shells could, and did, disinter them once more.

a short while some way behind our own lines. This was signalled to the batteries by the enemy planes turning sharply towards our lines. At the same time every enemy battery ceased firing during the time our aeroplanes were up. While enemy planes are observing from early morning to late in the evening, our own aeroplanes hardly ever venture near, although when they do come, the enemy aircraft retire for a short time.

The opinion is that our trenches cannot protect troops even during a barrage of the shortest duration owing to lack of dug-outs. The enemy understands how to prevent with his terrible barrage the bringing up of building material and even how to hinder the work itself. The consequence is that our trenches are vulnerable to an assault by the enemy.

Our artillery which does occasionally lay down a barrage on the enemy's trenches at a great expense of ammunition, cannot cause similar destruction to the enemy. He can bring his building material up, can repair his trenches as well as building new ones, can bring up rations and ammunition and remove the wounded etc. The continual barrage on our lines of communication make it very difficult for us to ration and relieve our troops, to supply water, ammunition, building material, evacuate wounded and causes heavy losses. This and the lack of protection from artillery fire and the weather, the lack of hot meals, the continual necessity of having to lie in the same place, the danger of being buried, the long time that the wounded have to remain in the trenches has a most demoralising effect on the troops. All this is due to the excellent air service directing the enemy's medium and heavy artillery fire.

Only with the greatest difficulty could the men be persuaded to stay in the trenches in these conditions.

Prisoners captured at 'Factory Corner'

They appear to be discontented and stated that the moment there was any word of going up into the line, their remaining officer and *feldwebel* reported themselves sick and they were led by a *faenrich* [officer cadet] who had not previously been in action and had no idea where they were or where they were going.

Captured German report of the fighting on the Somme

The British infantry are smart in attack, largely because of their immense confidence in their great artillery superiority. One must admit the skill with which they consolidate themselves in newly gained positions. They show great tenacity in defence. Small parties when once established with machine guns in the corner of a wood or a group of houses are very difficult to dislodge.

Hitherto our instructions from experience gained in defence and attack were based on a carefully constructed trench system. The troops on the Somme front found practically no trenches at all.

(The above sentence shows the effect of our artillery.)

Diary of a leutnant, 2nd Company, 180th Infantry Regiment 5 September 1916

Today at 2 pm we were relieved by the 66th and arrived at the south edge of Thiepval, in the Thiepval Riegel ['Bar']. Thus we are again exactly on the spot where we began the trench war.

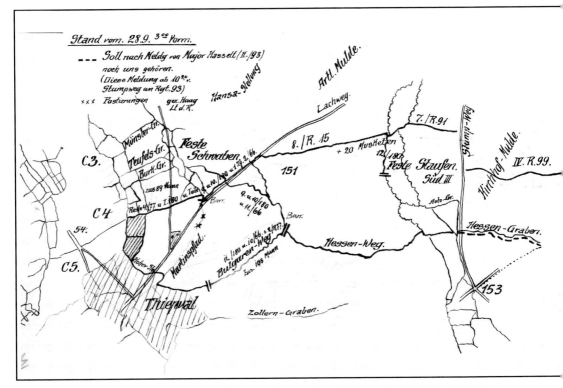

German map showing the situation at Thiepval on the morning of 28 September 1916. The British have captured the remains of the village. (The Germans at Thiepval by Jack Sheldon)

9 September 1916

To-day his excellency von Soden was here; he is proud that his division stands at the cardinal point of the offensive. 'If it were not for us Thiepval would be "English".'

22 September 1916

I have examined the position around me – it is a lost post. We see quite certainly at every advance of the English near Le Sars, and above all towards Miraumont is about to cause Thiepval to fall like a ripe fruit into their hands. The superiority of the English airmen and owing to the skill of their artillery oppresses one. At present only the airmen take the offensive and they are admirable. But in spite of all we must, and shall, win.

To-day the English are relieving in broad daylight and I could see them plainly causing me to secretly clench my fists. Depressing!

24 September 1916

Yesterday there was a bombardment of our trenches with guns of all calibres and it lasted many hours. The airmen circled above as if they were over an aerodrome, only these airmen have machine guns and use them.

I am wearing my gas mask as I write. The gas gets more and more troublesome. It got so strong that men fell ill.

25 September 1916

Our company commander Leutnant of the Reserve Lindmann, has reported sick, having been gassed. As next senior I have to take over the company. It is a difficult situation, I have to hold the threatened outpost, Thiepval, that is being assaulted on all sides and by every means. They are shelling the trenches with guns of all calibres. Today they bombarded the Second Line all afternoon. Every three or four minutes the dug-out quakes and the candles go out. One only sits and waits for the dug-out to be hit and caved in, or until evening comes.

Shortages in bandages – another indicator of the terrible toll being taken on life and limb. A casualty clearance station on the Somme.

German order – medical stores

Orders have been issued repeatedly that great economy must be practiced in the use of medical stores chiefly in casualty clearing stations and hospitals. Dressings are to be used several times, unless the patient has an infectious disease. There is a great shortage of

morphia and of pure aspirin. The latter is almost unprocurable and is to be replaced 'Ersatz Aspirin'. Iodine is scarce also chloroform and strict economy must be practiced with regard to the use of the latter.

Extract from an unposted letter from a man of the 21st Bavarian Regiment, 5th Bavarian Division

> Our present position is in the Lens neighbourhood – a very windy corner. The English are opposite us. The best that could happen would be for this swindle to come to an end. The Devil himself could not stick it here with these Englishmen. I am fed up. Every day there is less to eat and we are told to write home that we are happy and satisfied. I am giving this letter to a chap going home on leave; otherwise I would not have been able to write all this.

Some opinions

Prisoners are of the opinion that they were quite uselessly sacrificed in a hopeless task as a consequence their morale is very poor.

The Bavarians tore off their national cockade thinking that the British do not give quarter to Bavarians.

Extract from a diary of an officer of the 226th Minenwerfer Company

24 September 1916
Thiepval

> At 5 pm the enemy began bombarding Thiepval village and Schwaben Redoubt with heavy artillery and gas shells. The smell of gas was detected everywhere and forced the garrison soldiers to wear

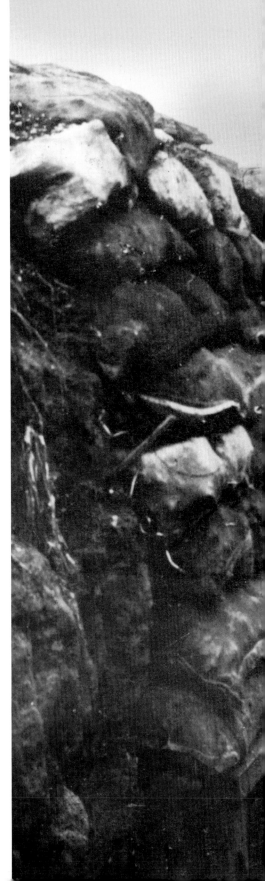

A medium trench mortar and team.

their gas helmets for more than two hours. The medium trench mortar in Brown Trench [Brauner Graben] was totally destroyed. The dug-out was full of men and there was considerable confusion among the machine gunners.

German order
September 1916

Brigades will submit a report on 25 September with regard to the Regimental supply of steel helmets. The XIV Reserve Corps has reported as follows:

Owing to the present shortage of steel helmets (these cannot be supplied from home [Germany] for the time being) directly a supply becomes available they will be distributed amongst Regiments south of the Ancre. No requests for steel helmets by troops other than infantry can be considered until all the infantry have been supplied.

German document
Group HQ employment of field guns
9 September 1916

Group Marschall
Section A. Nr. 4864/693
According to daily reports, so-called 'harassing fire' still continues to be carried out by day, contrary to the orders of the Chief of the General Staff of the Field Army.

If what is intended by this intermittent, methodical and accurately observed fire is the destruction of the enemy's trenches then, at the least, it is misguided. Targets of that nature are undertaken by both the heavy and light field howitzers, not the field guns. The field gun is best used against unconcealed targets where rapid employment is required. For this purpose it is essential for the battery commanders to have good observation and for the battery to have been registered, not only for laying down a barrage, but on all areas likely to be in use by the enemy. Should the enemy be able to move about in the rear areas throughout the battle zone with impunity, it shows evidence of incompetent observation. If, on the other hand, the expression referred to above means that the intention is to cause losses to the enemy whilst rebuilding work is being undertaken by him at night, and troops are being moved up to occupy the trenches, then field guns can be advantageously employed for that purpose.

Signed Frhr. Marschall

Civilian labour
Order of the III Bavarian Corps

21 September 1916

Civilian labour is to be used to the utmost possible extent, without regard to status, for any kind of work that will not actually take the civilians under fire, and especially for work in munitions factories well behind the front. A scale of wages is fixed for the civilian labour in the III Bavarian Corps District.

A captured official document shows that the German War Office has had to recall a large number of workmen from the ranks of the army in order to meet the requirements of the manufacture of war material.

Explosive bullets

Conclusive evidence has been obtained that explosive bullets were used by the Germans in the vicinity of Thiepval. About 500 rounds of the ammunition was discovered. On the body of a German officer a case of explosive ammunition was found, out of which eight rounds had been fired.

Extract from captured letters

To an officer of the 14th Bavarian Regiment
11 September 1916, Nurnberg
Dear...
We have seen the Prince [of Bavaria]. He was, however, very quiet and not very cheerful. The cheering was rather weak.

Prince Leopold reviewing Jäger and Saxon infantry. From the tone of a letter to an officer of the 14th Bavarian Regiment the royal Field Marshal's popularity was waning.

There is absolutely no more preserved meat and one is condemned to the eternal fish diet.

A letter written in the field: 180th Regiment, MG Company 26 September 1916

South of Thiepval

We relieved a machine gun crew who had the only entrance to the dug-out caved in by a gas shell. You can't imagine what misery this is. Our Company Commander was gassed and is now in hospital. The bombardment has again begun at a rate to make a man dizzy. I'm convinced that soon we will have either to withdraw or be taken by the English.

A letter by a man of 153rd Regiment

25 September 1916

North of Mouquet Farm

We are about an hour's distance from the front line, but yet so many shells come over that we are deafened and blinded. There are about fifty-six of us in a dug-out here. This is more than a bombardment, it sounds as if a thousand drums were playing and it is not surprising to hear that men are missing, for they are torn to pieces. Many are buried and never manage to dig themselves out again. It would be better if German women and girls could visit this place for the war would soon be over then.

153rd Regiment, Battalion Command Post

22 September 1916

[Probably Stuff Redoubt]

In the case of an attack we are not in a position to defend ourselves much less to mount a counter-attack. Our rifles have been dragged through the mud and are useless for firing. All we have are bayonets and hand grenades. I think that if the Tommies come now no one would put up a fight, the men would gladly surrender to them.

Chapter Five

Drawing to a Close, October 1916

Extract from No.24 Squadron RFC Record Book
1 October 1916

Attack on Faucourt-L'Abbaye

Lieutenant Byrne reached the line at 4.15 pm. From 4.15 to 5.50 he continually flew over the area Faucourt-L'Abbaye – Le Sars at an average height of 800 feet and successfully carried out a tactical reconnaissance. His machine was badly damaged by rifle fire from the ground being hit in thirty different places and some of the instruments shot away. On two occasions, once at M12a45 and again at M11c.75, he descended to 500 feet and fired a complete double drum into reinforcements coming up causing a great deal of casualties and confusion.

British attack on Le Sars

An Albatros CIII over a forest somewhere in France. German infantry in the trenches were loud in their criticism of their comrades in the Air Force to protect them from the Royal Flying Corps and the French Service Aéronautique.

7 October 1916

1.10 pm. Lieutenant Barnes and Second Lieutenant Hartley, No 34 Squadron RFC dropped cards (calling on the enemy to surrender and promising him kind treatment) on Le Sars, Le Barque and Ligny Thilloy. (Observer wounded in the arm by machine-gun fire at 2.10 pm.)

Extract from No.34 Squadron record book
9 October 1916

At 8.45 am Lieutenant Byrne encountered seven H.A. (hostile aircraft) over Le Transloy at 2,000 feet, he flew towards them firing bursts at 300 yards range. The H.A. split up, five going south-east

A British officer of the Intelligence Corps interrogating a German prisoner shortly after his capture.

and two going north. Lieutenant B. attacked the latter machines getting to within one hundred yards

range and driving them off. He then engaged the remaining five. After 25 minutes fighting he drove them east.

It is reported that enemy aeroplanes make a practice of firing their machine guns when there are none of our aeroplanes about simply to make our troops run out to observe the fight in the air and in this way can find what gun pits etc are occupied.

Prisoner of the 12th Company, 7th Bavarian Regiment, 5th Bavarian Division
6 October 1916

Prisoner was captured in the front line and states that he moved there on the night of 9/10th September relieving the II Battalion. He is nineteen years old and belongs to the 1917 Class. He was called up 19 January 1916 in Bayreuth and says that he was sent to join the 7th Regiment near St Mihiel in July. He claims to be one of the first of this class to be called up in the district. There are, it seems, about ten men of this class in the 12th Company.

Translation of a report by Leube (NCO)
9 October 1916

To Company Commander Leutnant Busch, 9th Company, 66th Reserve Infantry Regiment.

This afternoon at 2 o'clock I paraded the entire Company at Bertincourt. I read out from the sick list all the names of the sick and seven men whom the doctor considered fit for trench duty. I ordered them to fall out and said, 'Get your packs ready, you go into the line this afternoon.' All paraded at the Orderly Room at 4.45 pm whereupon Rifleman Person stepped

Farm at Bertincourt where two men of the 66th Reserve Infantry Regiment refused to return to the trenches.

forward and said, 'I refuse to go into the line' and was followed by Rifleman Weber who said, 'I also refuse to go into the line.' I pointed out to both of them what the consequences of refusing to move into the line would bring. Whereupon Rifleman Person said, 'I had already thought it over for two days'. Rifleman Weber said, 'I can't go into the line.' I have ordered both to be placed under arrest in the guard room at Bertincourt.

Signed Kamfrath, Oberfeldwebel.

Enemy precautions against tanks

The following extract from a battalion order captured in the Ancre sector contained the first reference by the enemy for methods of dealing with tanks.

a. The Companies are responsible for the repair and upkeep of the wire entanglements in front of their sectors.

b. In view of danger of attacks by English tanks all roads leading from our positions, and not used for the passage of traffic and artillery, are to be dug out for a width of four to six metres and to a depth of one and half to two metres. A narrow way being left for the passage of infantry and supplies. In addition all these roads must be obstructed so as to render traffic, except the passage of material impossible.

By 7.30 am tomorrow the Companies will report that this work has been completed.

Officer of the 11th Reserve Infantry Regiment

He states that drafts come up rapidly and in sufficient numbers, but that the men are young and poorly trained. He said that he would sooner have one platoon of men over forty than two platoons of these young recruits who are very jumpy and apt to get out of hand in a critical situation. The officer is a regular of five years service. He said that Thiepval was always considered impregnable and that its fall made a great impression, particularly on old soldiers who knew the place.

Extract from a German official publication
Nahkampfmittel **(Weapons for Close Combat)**
7 August 1916.
This indicates that the Germans are giving up the manufacture of rifle grenades.

The rifle grenade owing to its want of accuracy (wind etc)

Rifle grenade on a specially designed stand which could be turned to aim the projectile. From the document dated 7 August 1916 employment of this trench weapon was to be discontinued.

accomplishes little other than annoying the enemy, rather than obtaining any real effect. No more rifle grenades will, therefore, be manufactured. They are best employed to provide flanking fire, to cover dead ground and to produce a heavy searching fire on large areas etc.

German casualties

The total number of German casualties exclusive of naval or colonial casualties reported up to the end of September in official German lists is 3,556,018.

The figures for September 1916 and totals are as follows:

Killed and died of wounds	30,306	817,560
Died of sickness	1,976	52,622
Prisoners	1,839	178,862
Missing	30,420	249,967
Severely wounded	25,786	478,854
Wounded	6,482	280,880
Slightly wounded	69,804	1,318,834
Wounded remaining with units	13,271	178,439
Total	179,884	3,556,018

Captured message
13 October 1916

The following message was brought in by a man of the III Battalion, 64th Regiment, who wandered into our lines yesterday morning.

Sender	Notice	Place	Date	Time
III/64th	Left Batt	Firing Line	13.10.16	1.05 am

Arrived

To II/64th

1. Apparently the machine guns of 'Martins' platoon have fallen into the hands of the enemy.
2. Of the remaining guns of the 2nd MG Company, only one remains.
3. Of the infantry company there is no sign.
4. The position is untenable. I beg therefore that the company of the II Battalion should immediately be ordered to assist.

In the event of the non-arrival of a company of the II/64th by, at the latest two hours before dawn, both the III/64th along with the 24th Infantry Regiment, which is on the right, will likely be overwhelmed by an enemy flank attack. It is imperative that the machine guns of the I Battalion be brought into the line in this sector.

13 October 1916

A prisoner captured on the 13th states that in private life he was a waiter. Before the outbreak of war he was employed at the Charing Cross Hotel and the Strand Palace Hotel.

Tanks

Deserters from the I Battalion, 86th Reserve Infantry Regiment, 18th Reserve Division, captured by the army formations on our right had heard that the next entry of our tanks into their front line would be met by bombing attacks from the rear of the tank, directed against the driving band.

Instructions on how to deal with the new British weapon that had suddenly appeared on the Western Front was being passed around – immobilise it by blowing off the tracks at the back. This MkI is passing through a burning village.

Extract from RFC Squadron record book
15 October 1916

No.9 Squadron. Second Lieutenant Macdonald A.
10.30 am. Observed about one company of infantry in main street of Le Transloy at N30.b. 0000 going east. Dived down to 200 feet and fired two drums into them. Company dispersed in all directions; several figures being left in the street.

The buildings and streets of Le Transloy. The village was part of the German strong defensive system which included the villages of Les Boeufs, Morval and Combles. When the Somme battles ended it was still in German hands.

German document

362nd Infantry Regiment Commandant Bapaume B. Nr.1570 I

Order for the construction of defences at Bapaume

3 October 1916

1. The defences of Bapaume will be divided into the Northern Sub-Sector from the Bapaume-Bienvillers road to the Bapaume-Thilloy road. Southern Sub-Sector. Joining up with the above and extending as far as the Bapaume-Rancourt road. Hauptmann Welter will be in charge of the defence work in the Northern Sub-Sector, and Hauptmann Hagenmann of that in the Southern Sub-Sector.

A German observation balloon tethered over the occupied town of Bapaume. In the event of an Allied break-through the town was to be defended like a fortress.

A German military band choses a position in front of the statue to General Louis Faidherbe in the Grande Place, Bapaume, to play its martial music. Faidherbe gained fame in the Franco-Prussian War of 1870–71 when, as commander of the Army of the North, he won victories against the invading Prussian army. Bapaume was the goal of the Allies in their 1916 offensive on the Somme. Civilians were still in the town in June, but as shells heavy shelling began they were evacuated.

2. Until further orders, each of these officers will have two companies of II/362 at his disposal. The Sub-Sector commanders will arrange for each company to be allotted a definite sector of the work, for which the Company Commander will be responsible. I will order further working parties from the four platoons and from the men fit for garrison duty who are in Bapaume to assist in this work as may be necessary. These specially detailed working parties will only work under the orders of the Sub-Sector and Company Commanders (working hours 6 am to 8 pm in two shifts).

3. The construction of dug-outs and obstacles is to be undertaken first of all. In every Company Sector, which will be about 550 yards long, work on ten dug-outs is to be begun at once. (Roomy dug-outs to accommodate two groups (sixteen men) with two exits each. In all new trenches the traverses must be at least nineteen and a half feet wide.

4. Leutnant Meyer, Machine Gun Officer, will (independently of the work of the Sub-Sector Commanders) arrange for machine gun emplacements along the whole defensive front. These should provide flanking fire and so far as possible, be sited at commanding points behind the line. For this purpose the 1st and 3rd Machine Gun Companies are placed at his disposal.

5. Entrenching tools are to be drawn from the tool wagons. Further tools and material are to be requested from Leutnant Henke, 4th Company, XIV Pioneer Battalion in South Bapaume.
Signed von Hugo
Major and Regimental Commander

Street off the Square leading to the village of Péronne is being wrecked.

Morale of the 24th Division

When it was known that the 24th Division was to come back to the Somme, the older men of the 133rd Regiment were very depressed, stating that they would prefer to be shot on the spot rather than go back there and sincerely hoping that they might be taken prisoner.

Extract from a letter
8 October 1916

Auhausen

To a man of the 15th Bavarian Infantry Regiment

Tomorrow the 9th, the 1918 Class are going to be called up.

Extract from a diary
Monday 9 October 1916

A man belonging to 64th Regiment, 6th Division

Our Company Commander has sprained [*verstaugt zu*] his foot and reported sick. The Battalion Commander has also reported sick. Now Leutnant Droysen is commanding the battalion and Hauptmann Hildebrande the four platoons in reserve. That is what happens if the shell-proof dug-outs fail, but, as for the rest of us, we have to put up with it.

German map showing the British and German trench lines from Flers to Bapaume.

21 October 1916

Bombs were dropped on Corbie and Querrieu in the morning (3 am).

A part of the ancient medieval defences at Bapaume during the occupation by the Germans. The Alte Befestigung *were totally unsuited for Twentieth Century use.*

Extracts from an account of a British soldier who took part in the British attack of 17/18th October

He remained in the German line until the night of the 18/19th. He was on the right flank of his battalion and entered Sunken Road at N.20d. 1535. At this point there is a small barricade of boxes and earth. This was manned by one German whom he shot. Other dead Germans were lying in the road. In the banks of the road were several dug-outs, considerably knocked about.

A few minutes later the road, which has a trench on both sides, was manned by a large party of Germans (estimated by him at 100) who fired from the road both east and west. Finding himself alone he crawled into the sap at N20d.1035, and remained there hiding in a blown in dug-out.

The sap and sunken road are defended by two coils of concertina wire which is not pegged down. The coils extended as far as could be seen in front of Bayonet Trench. During the day the sunken road was manned by five Germans. At night it was thickly held. The army sent up a large number of Very lights and appeared nervous. He heard a large number talking in another trench behind, about sixty yards (Bayonet Trench). It was from this trench that all the lights went up. He crawled out of the west end of the sap at 7.30 and reached our lines.

Friction between Bavarians and Prussians
13 October 1916

Extract from a letter by a man of the 7th Bavarian Regiment, 5th Bavarian Division

It looks as though you are about to be moved, or have you already left? All the German troops are being sent to the Somme. This much is certain, you can see no Prussians there and this is in spite of the losses the I Bavarian Corps suffered at Verdun recently. And how

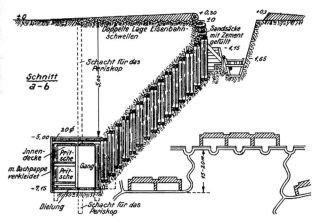

Left a German diagram for constructing underground shelters.
Right: An underground field kitchen (note the layers of logs and use of steel girders for the roof.
Bottom left: sheltering inside Bapaume church and (bottom right) the destruction of that building by British shell fire.

Three 'old soldiers' returning to their unit following a period of leave.

we did suffer! It appears that we are in for another turn; at least the 5th Bavarian Division.

Everybody has been talking about it for a long time. To the Devil with it! Every Bavarian Regiment is being sent into it. It's a swindle! The Prussians say that it is a hot corner.

Extract from a letter

18 October 1916

Man in hospital from the 161st Regiment, 185th Division, to a man of the 396th Regiment

Cille, Germany

You will wonder at my being in Germany. Our Regiment was suddenly taken from Flanders and flung into the Somme sector. Twelve days we stayed there and were completely smashed up. Ten days I endured that hell and then came to the end of my strength and became sick with Enteric and was put on the next transport for Germany.

On the 13th or 23rd I shall be discharged and come to Eschweiler to the Ersatz Battalion.

On the Somme front; recently completed concrete dug-outs smashed by British artillery.

Wastage of enemy's artillery material

A captured letter, written by a man of the 13th Artillery Regiment states that during eight weeks his battery fired 34,000 rounds and used up twenty-eight guns. Of these, eleven were damaged by overheating of the bore and seventeen were knocked out by British artillery fire.

Extracts from a conversation with a captured officer
2nd Company, I Battalion, 104th Infantry Regiment, 40th Saxon Division
20 October 1916

The officer was captured in Snag Trench as he was returning to Tail Trench to ask for reinforcements and also to get help for his Company Commander who was wounded. He lost his way and finding himself suddenly surrounded on three sides was forced to surrender. Since coming into the line their losses had been extremely heavy, but the proportion of killed was small.

They all think that our offensive is at an end and that we cannot pursue it throughout the winter. He thought that the English had the power to go on for ever, but not the other Allies.

German attack on Schwaben Redoubt
20 October

The importance the Germans attached to this attack is shown by the following extract from a Regimental Order of the 109th Reserve Infantry Regiment.

> In case this has not already been done the men are to be informed by their immediate superiors that this attack is not merely a matter of re-taking a trench because it was formerly in German possession, but that the recapture of an extremely important point is involved. If the enemy remains on the ridge he can blow all our artillery in the Ancre Valley to pieces and the protection for our infantry will thus be destroyed.
>
> Any man capturing an English soldier will be granted fourteen days' leave.

22 October 1916

> During the morning the Germans shelled their own trenches opposite M24 central. Rockets were sent up falling into three stars, a signal to his artillery to lengthen the range.

German attack near Schwaben Redoubt
22 October 1916

> During this attack it is reported that while the Germans waved their hands as though they wished to surrender, snipers were waiting to pick off any of our men who exposed themselves – an old German trick.

Extract from a diary
A man of the 111th Reserve Regiment, 28th Reserve Division

> We entrained at Savigny and at once knew our destination – our old blood bath – the Somme.
>
> We relieved the 119th Reserve Infantry Regiment on 7 October and had dreadful casualties that night: the 9th Company dwindled to twenty-nine men; two platoons were taken prisoner and the rest were buried in the dug-outs. We (the 10th Company) have already lost thirty men.

Reichstag Session – some typical extracts
October 1916

Herr Bassermann, National Liberal:
The will to victory in the German army remains unbroken. Confidence in the German Command is unshaken. Peace can only be expected from a beaten enemy. The brilliant result of the War Loan proves the justness of our financial policy, as well as the united resolution of the nation to persevere to final victory.

Herr Spahn, Centre:
We shall be victorious on the battlefield and victorious at home economically. Great Britain is the worst and most scheming of all our enemies. The tent of the War Lords, according to Napoleon's words, must first be destroyed if victory is to be obtained.

Count Westarp, Conservative:
The War Loan has afforded a glorious proof that the people stand united behind the Army in its determination to achieve victory.

Grand words from Germany's politicians in the seat of government, the Reichstag, but, by the end of 1916, many of the families in that country were ill-clad and malnourished and with two more years ahead of them.

British prisoners taken in the fighting for the Schwaben Redoubt in October 1916. Condition of the road indicates deteriorating weather as the Somme battles came to a close. The urgent need for Somme intelligence gathering dwindled.